Build Wealth Through Property: 7 Reasons Why

HOW PROPERTY CREATES FINANCIAL FREEDOM & SECURITY

By Christopher Ifonlaja

First edition 2026

Printed in United Kingdom

C&A Publishing

ISBN: 978-1-9194487-0-1

Dedication

To God, who ordered my footsteps and guided my path with purpose — to You be all the glory.

To my parents, for the values you instilled, the sacrifices you made, and the foundation you laid long before I understood its importance.

To my family, for your patience, belief, and unwavering support through every season.

Acknowledgements

No book is ever written alone. First and foremost, I give thanks to God for inspiring this work and helping me to make it a reality.

I would like to acknowledge Lanre Osibona, whose insight and encouragement at a pivotal moment helped inspire the beginning of my property journey. What appeared to be an ordinary meeting on Fore Street, Edmonton in London proved to be anything but chance.

My sincere thanks to Roger Courtney, whose thoughtful review and constructive feedback were invaluable to this work. His wisdom and honest critique were very helpful.

Special thanks to Oluchi Nwaiwu for her exceptional diligence, editorial insight, and careful attention to detail in refining this manuscript. Her commitment to clarity and substance was instrumental in bringing this work to its final form.

My deepest gratitude goes to my wife, Angela, who not only supported this work but also walks the investment journey alongside me, offering encouragement, wisdom, and unwavering belief throughout.

I would also like to sincerely thank Victor Olorunshola for his careful verification of the figures in this book, and TG Sabastine for the cover design.

Many thanks to Sharon Fiberesima for her support in preparing the manuscript for print. Her responsiveness and professionalism helped bring this project across the line.

I would also like to extend my heartfelt appreciation to my niece, Oreoluwa Bammeke, for her attention to detail in reviewing the final print layout. Her thoughtful observations and contributions were greatly valued.

Finally, to the reader, thank you for picking up this book. My hope is that it helps you think clearly, act wisely, and approach property not merely as an investment, but as a long-term tool for stability, freedom, and responsible stewardship.

Chris Ifonlaja

Critical Disclaimer

This book outlines strategic principles designed to help reduce investment risk when applied correctly. These principles do not guarantee success.

Property investment involves financial risk. Market values can fall, rental income may stop, and investors can lose money. I have personally experienced both profitable and unprofitable outcomes, and this book reflects lessons learned from both.

Applying these principles with discipline, informed decision-making, and sound risk management can significantly lower the likelihood of major losses, but it does not eliminate the possibility of financial loss. Individual results will vary, and past performance is not an indicator of future returns.

Before making any investment decisions, you should seek advice from qualified and regulated professionals, such as:

- An Independent Financial Adviser (FCA regulated)
- A Property Solicitor or Conveyancer
- A Qualified Accountant
- A Mortgage Broker

I am not regulated by the Financial Conduct Authority (FCA), and I do not provide regulated financial advice. This book offers educational material and personal experiences only. I do not accept any liability for losses, damages, or adverse outcomes resulting from the use or misuse of the information presented in this book.

By continuing to read, you acknowledge that you understand and accept these caveats.

Contents

Preface

How it all started...

By the age of twenty-two, when I bought my first property, owning a home, let alone earning income from one, felt far-fetched. Property ownership seemed reserved for people far more established than I was. That perception changed one afternoon when I ran a slightly older former schoolmate on Fore Street in Edmonton, London. After exchanging pleasantries, with Lanre Osibona,I asked what he was doing in the area.

"A viewing," he replied.

"A viewing for what?"

"Houses for purchase."

That simple answer quietly altered my financial thinking. It sparked a curiosity that led me into ongoing learning about property, a journey that continues to this day. In property, knowledge is not abstract. It produces results.

At the time, I did not know anyone who owned property in the UK. My parents owned their home elsewhere, and I had no understanding of how the process worked. I assumed property ownership was something only much older people pursued. My focus, like that of my friends, was education, work, and enjoying life. Weekends, and sometimes weekdays, revolved around bars and nightclubs. Saving for a deposit was not a priority. We lived as though the future would somehow take care of itself.

That mindset remains common today. Many people spend significant time and money travelling the world, chasing experiences and appearances in pursuit of social validation, often measured through social media approval – likes and shares, while lacking a clear financial strategy or long-term direction. Travel has value, but it becomes far more powerful when paired with intention and foresight.

When I asked, "Is it really that easy to own property?" Lanre smiled and said, "Yes."

"Where do you find properties?"

"Estate agents."

"And how can you afford one?"

"A mortgage. Go to your bank and speak to an estate agent."

It felt like a crash course delivered in a single conversation.

Coincidentally, there was a bank on the same street, called Abbey National, now Santander. I already had an account with them, so I booked an appointment and, before long, secured a mortgage with the bank. With my savings (I saved more) and with the help of a solicitor and an estate agent, I bought my first property. It was a modest ex-local authority two-bedroom split-level apartment in Enfield, London.

At the time, I lived at my aunt's place and hardly paid rent. With the bank's permission, I rented out the apartment through an estate agent on a guaranteed rent scheme[1] and received a fixed income whether the property was occupied or not. That same agent still manages one or two properties for me today.

Each month, income arrived without additional work. For a young man, earning money legitimately, without drugs or fraud, was intoxicating. The income eased financial pressure, but its impact went deeper. I felt more responsible, productive, and progressive. I felt liberated. From that moment on, I was hooked.

That experience changed everything. Until then, property income had been theoretical. Now it was real. I realised property could be

---

[1] A guaranteed rent scheme is an arrangement where a third party agrees to pay a fixed rental income to a property owner for a set period regardless of occupancy, often in exchange for managing the property, though this may involve lower returns, reduced control, and contractual risks.

more than shelter. It could be a working asset, creating independence and opening options I had never seriously considered.

Looking back on that meeting on Fore Street, I now see how pivotal it was. Interestingly, the boarding school we both attended had the motto "Knowledge is light." That day, I discovered just how true that statement was.

My hope is that what you gain from this book will be just as illuminating.

Welcome to your journey in property investment. Let us begin, one property at a time.

WHAT TO EXPECT FROM THIS BOOK

Build Wealth Through Property: 7 Reasons Why is designed to provide clarity, confidence, and a structured framework for building wealth through property. Its purpose is not simply to inform, but to equip you with the mindset and discipline required to think like a property investor strategically, analytically, and with conviction.

Throughout these pages, you will develop a clear understanding of the fundamentals that underpin successful property investment, organised around seven core reasons that explain why, when approached correctly, failure is not inevitable.

You will explore proven strategies, real-life case studies, and practical tools that support consistent, long-term success. The focus is not on theory alone, but on translating informed decisions into sustainable outcomes.

WHO THIS BOOK IS FOR

This book is written for anyone who wants to take deliberate control of their financial future through property investment. Whether you are new to property, exploring your first purchase, seeking to build a portfolio, or refining an existing strategy, the principles in this book are designed to meet you where you are.

It will resonate with homeowners curious about turning property into an income-generating asset, professionals seeking to diversify income streams, and experienced investors looking to sharpen their approach through deeper understanding of structure, leverage, and strategy.

If you have ever wondered how property can create wealth, protect against inflation, and provide long-term financial security, this book is written with you in mind. It is practical, grounded in real experience, and intended to provoke thoughtful action.

HOW THIS BOOK IS STRUCTURED

Part 1: Foundations (Chapters 1-3)

These chapters provide a framework for thinking about values and risk, supporting wiser and more sustainable investment decisions.

Following the preface, the book opens with a foundational introduction to property investment, followed by a chapter on stewardship and risk as the framework for responsible and sustainable investing. From there, it unfolds into two distinct sections.

Part 2: The 7 Wealth Drivers (Chapters 4-10)

These chapters explain the seven core reasons property builds long-term wealth, using practical examples and real-world insights.

The first section explores the core principles that underpin successful property investment and explains why property has remained a powerful wealth-building vehicle across generations. These chapters examine the pathways property offers, including income generation, capital leverage, long-term appreciation, inflation hedging, value preservation, and tax efficiency. Together, they present property not merely as an asset, but as a strategic platform for building long-term wealth and legacy.

Part 3: Execution and Tools (Chapters 11-13)

These chapters focus on implementation: building your team, understanding the numbers, taking your first steps, and using checklists and templates to stay organised

The next section moves from understanding to application. The focus shifts to the practical realities of investing well, assembling the right professional team, understanding the numbers behind real transactions, and navigating the purchasing process with clarity and confidence. This section is designed to bridge the gap between knowledge and execution.

Each chapter builds deliberately on the one before it, creating a clear progression from foundational insight to practical action. By prioritising understanding before tactics, the book equips readers to assess opportunities objectively, manage risk appropriately, and take informed, confident steps toward building and sustaining their own property portfolio.

Chapter 1 Understanding Property Investment

"Rome wasn't built in a day, but they were laying bricks every hour."[2] — Proverb (often attributed to John Heywood)

What if your income was no longer limited to the hours, you could personally work? What if, over time, your assets began to contribute to your income rather than relying entirely on your time and effort? For many people, property investment represents that possibility. Not overnight wealth. Not effortless income. But a practical pathway to long-term security and wealth.

Property has quietly shaped wealth, stability, and opportunity for many people over time. Across cultures and economic cycles, it has remained one of the few assets that people not only desire but consistently depend upon. Yet despite its familiarity, property investment is often misunderstood, either dismissed as unattainable or oversold as effortless.

This book was written to cut through both extremes and present a balanced, practical view of property investment. It is intended to

---

[2] The proverb "Rome was not built in one day" appears in John Heywood, A Dialogue Containing the Number in Effect of All the Proverbs in the English Tongue (1546). The extended wording used here is a modern adaptation.

inspire people of all ages to recognise the power and possibilities property can offer. Property investment is not reserved for the rich or the powerful.

For those who believe they are too young, that is simply not true. Ownership requires income, savings, affordability, and financial responsibility, and the earlier these principles are understood, the sooner financial discipline can begin. Others feel it's not for them because they are new to an environment or believe they are only passing through. Before writing yourself off, gain knowledge, understand your context, ask the right questions, and avoid assumptions. Life sometimes has a different plan for us.

Property, when managed well, is more than a source of extra income. It has the capacity to replace earned income and support financial independence for those willing to learn, plan, and act. While other routes exist, such as building a business, growing a platform, or advancing a career, property stands out for its accessibility and durability. It is as much about mindset and persistence as it is about money and numbers. Challenges are inevitable, but each one strengthens judgment and capability. There are no slogans or shortcuts. Property rewards foresight, disciplined saving, sound strategy, and patience, becoming not just an investment, but a system that supports long-term goals.

Before committing this book to print, I shared my story with many people, particularly young people, because of the power of time and compounding—the way small, consistent gains can grow significantly over time—in property investment. In doing so, I challenged stereotypes and helped people see possibilities differently. One example that particularly delighted me was a young lady I encouraged to purchase her apartment. She was afraid and wanted to wait for the "right time." She eventually went ahead and bought, later telling me the turning point was when I shared my favourite property quote, "You don't wait to buy property; you buy property and wait."

There is also the young man who went on to make his first purchase at the age of twenty-one after he saw what I was doing as a young adult. The same goes for even more established adults who I shared with, who had disposable income but didn't quite appreciate the opportunities and the possibilities around property investment. Property, when acquired in the right place and structured correctly, can serve as a haven, preserving wealth, generating stability, and supporting the transfer of legacy across generations.

This chapter establishes the foundation for understanding property investment. It explains what property investment is, why property functions as a durable and widely relied-upon asset, and how it differs from operating a traditional business. By clarifying these distinctions at the outset, the chapter equips you to approach property with the correct mindset, assess risk realistically, and understand how income, value, and involvement interact before considering strategy or tactics.

Property occupies a unique position as an asset class. It underpins daily life across societies, serving as housing, workplaces, places of worship, centres of trade, and spaces where communities form. Few assets are so deeply embedded in how society functions, which is why property has remained a consistent source of security, stability, and opportunity over time.

This universal reliance gives property investment its enduring strength. Owning an asset that people will always need and consistently demand is not speculative; it is strategic. Property is not merely a vehicle for profit, but a foundational asset positioned at the intersection of necessity, resilience, and long-term wealth creation.

Property investment, also known as real estate investing, is the intentional purchase, ownership, management, rental, or sale of property for profit. At its core, it involves owning an asset and leveraging its utility, demand, and value to generate income, growth, or both. For this reason, property remains one of the most accessible and time-tested paths to building long-term wealth.

For generations, property has been recognised as a cornerstone of financial independence and stability. It rewards those who think strategically, plan carefully, and remain patient. Success in property is not about luck, but about knowledge, timing, and disciplined execution.

Yet despite its familiarity, many people who engage with property for profit misunderstand what it represents from an investment perspective. Is it a business that demands constant attention, or an asset that works quietly in the background? To answer this clearly, it is important to distinguish between property as an investment and property as a business.

PROPERTY AS AN INVESTMENT VS PROPERTY AS A BUSINESS

As an asset class, property differs fundamentally from a traditional business. A business typically involves active, ongoing operations, producing goods or services, managing staff, and driving daily sales. Income is tied directly to continual effort and operational performance. Property investment, by contrast, is primarily about ownership of a property asset to generate returns through rental income, capital appreciation, or both, often with limited day-to-day involvement.

At its core, property is an investment, not a business. Once a property is acquired and correctly structured, it can generate returns without the level of daily involvement that most businesses demand. A property can take on business characteristics when it is scaled or operated in specific ways. The key distinction is not the nature of the asset itself, but how it is managed and the intensity of activity applied to it.

Portfolio ownership illustrates this clearly. Owning multiple properties introduces the need for systems to manage tenants, schedule maintenance, ensure compliance, and track cash flow. At this point, the investor is no longer simply holding assets, but overseeing a structured operation, even though the properties themselves remain investments.

Short-term and serviced accommodation push this dynamic further. Platforms such as Airbnb and Booking.com introduce a more operational model, requiring marketing, dynamic pricing, customer service, and frequent tenant turnover. A traditional rental property may experience one or two tenant changes over a decade, while serviced accommodation may see several guest turnovers in a single week. This level of activity requires defined processes and consistent oversight, causing the property to function more like a hospitality business than a passive investment.

Property development demonstrates the same principle at a different scale. A property acquired for development begins as an investment asset, valued for its land, location, and future potential. As the development progresses, involvement intensifies. The investor becomes responsible for budgeting, project management, contractor coordination, timelines, and risk control. At this stage, outcomes depend heavily on operational discipline and decision-making.

Despite this operational intensity, the foundation remains investment led. The result is still a property asset, enhanced through value creation. Additional profit arises not only from market movement, but from the operational value introduced along the way. Once the activity concludes, whether through sale, refinance, or stabilisation, the business layer recedes, leaving behind either a realised gain or a higher-quality investment asset.

A two-bedroom apartment in a city centre illustrates this distinction clearly. When held passively, it functions as a long-term rental, generating steady income with minimal day-to-day involvement while benefiting from capital appreciation, although not always. When operated actively through short-term bookings, the same apartment becomes a trading operation. Dynamic pricing, structured cleaning, and guest services shift performance away from market forces alone and towards systems and execution.

MANAGING RISK

While property offers flexibility and opportunity, it is not without risk. The same characteristics that make property powerful can magnify mistakes when decisions are rushed or poorly informed. For every success story, there are cautionary tales of loss. Many investors enter property lured by online hype or unrealistic expectations, only to discover the cost of inadequate preparation.

Property investment can deliver strong returns, but values can rise and fall. The warning is simple but essential: the value of your investment can go down as well as up, and you may not recover the full amount invested. Property should therefore be approached as a long-term journey, not a quick win, even though occasional short-term opportunities may arise.

Understanding risk is not meant to discourage, but to reinforce the importance of preparation and learning. Property consistently rewards those who take time to understand markets, plan carefully, and make informed decisions. The difference between success and disappointment is rarely luck. It is knowledge applied with discipline. To this end, chapter 3 is dedicated to Risk.

KNOWLEDGE IS PROFIT

Every successful investor shares one defining trait: a commitment to lifelong learning. Property markets evolve constantly, shaped by economic cycles, legislation, lending criteria, taxation, and changing patterns of demand. Investors who stay informed are better positioned to identify opportunities, avoid costly mistakes, and adapt as conditions change.

Knowledge in property is not abstract theory. It directly influences decision-making, negotiation strength, risk management, and ultimately profitability. In this sense, knowledge is not just power. It produces results.

With this foundation in place, we can now explore the broader landscape of property investment and the multiple pathways it offers.

INVESTOR PROFILES

With a clear separation between the different ways one can engage in property, investors can choose an approach that aligns with their available time, capacity, and level of interest. Property does not demand a single mode of participation. Rather, it allows investors to determine how actively they wish to be involved, based on their goals, lifestyle, and risk tolerance.

Some investors prefer simplicity and time freedom. Others are drawn to scale and optimisation of income, costs, and processes. Still others choose to make property their primary business. These differences are not a matter of right or wrong, but of fit. Understanding where you sit allows you to invest with clarity rather than comparison.

INVESTOR ARCHETYPES

The Passive Investor

The Passive Investor engages in property primarily as an investment rather than a business. This profile often suits individuals with demanding careers, businesses, or other commitments who prefer minimal day-to-day involvement.

Their approach typically involves purchasing property in carefully selected locations and delegating ongoing management to professional property managers or estate agents. The focus is on stable cash flow, prudent asset management, and long-term capital growth.

The strength of this archetype lies in consistency and longevity. The trade-off is less scope to increase income through hands-on management, in exchange for simplicity and time freedom. If you're a Passive Investor, your focus will be the single-let Buy-To-Let

(BTL[3]) market.

The Portfolio Builder

The Portfolio Builder occupies the space between passive ownership and active operation. Property is a serious wealth-building focus, though not always the investor's sole occupation.

This archetype builds and oversees multiple properties, often using systems and professional teams to maintain performance and compliance. While involvement is higher than that of a passive investor, the underlying mindset remains investment-led rather than operationally intensive.

The strength of the Portfolio Builder lies in scalability and balance. The trade-off is the need for structure, oversight, and increasing management capability as the portfolio grows. If you're a Portfolio Builder, you may consider Houses in Multiple Occupation (HMOs[4]), multiple BTL and perhaps apartment blocks.

The Active Operator

The Active Operator treats property as a primary business and applies a high level of involvement to accelerate returns. This archetype is commonly associated with development, refurbishment, and serviced accommodation.

The focus is on value creation through execution. This includes managing projects, pricing strategies, timelines, and operational performance. While the potential returns are higher, so too are the

---

[3] Buy-to-Let (BTL) refers to a property investment strategy in which residential property is purchased with the primary intention of renting it out to tenants in order to generate rental income. Buy-to-let properties are typically financed using specialist buy-to-let mortgages, where lending decisions are based largely on the property's rental income rather than the borrower's personal earnings.

[4] House in Multiple Occupation (HMO) is a residential property investment model where accommodation is let to multiple unrelated tenants on individual agreements, with shared communal facilities. HMOs can generate higher rental yields than single-let properties but carry increased management complexity and are subject to enhanced regulatory, licensing, and compliance obligations.

demands on time, expertise, and risk management.

The strength of the Active Operator is speed and control over outcomes. The trade-off is greater complexity and operational exposure.

These archetypes are not fixed identities but positions along a spectrum. Many investors move between them over time as their circumstances, experience, and objectives evolve.

UNDERSTANDING THE PROPERTY PURCHASE TIMELINE

For those new to property investment, it is important to understand that buying a property is not a quick process. It requires patience, preparation, and the ability to work through multiple stages that often take several months to complete. From the moment you decide to invest to the day you finally receive the keys, the process typically takes four to six months, and in some cases longer.

Below is a simplified timeline to help set realistic expectations:

Month 1 – Preparation and Strategy

Clarify your investment goal, budget, and deposit strategy. Build an adequate cash buffer and ensure you understand your borrowing capacity by reviewing your credit position[5] and lending criteria through a financial adviser.

Month 2 – Finance and Area Selection

Secure an Agreement in Principle (AIP) with a lender (Bank) by working with a mortgage broker and shortlist two to three target areas based on affordability, demand, and long-term fundamentals.

---

[5] Your credit position can be assessed by reviewing your credit report through recognised UK credit reference agencies such as Experian, Equifax, or TransUnion, which provide insight into credit history, outstanding commitments, and lender affordability indicators.

Month 3 – Viewing and Offer Stage

Begin viewing suitable properties, refine your criteria as needed, and submit offers on appropriate opportunities.

Month 4–6 – Legal and Transactional Process

Progress through surveys, conveyancing, mortgage offer, exchange of contracts, and completion. This is often the longest and least predictable stage of the process.

First 30 Days After Completion

Arrange insurance, complete statutory compliance checks, and onboard tenants if the property is being let.

For practical support at each stage, refer to the Appendices for detailed checklists and templates designed to guide you through the process step by step.

CONCLUSION

Property occupies a distinctive position between investment and business. At its core, it is an asset capable of generating income, preserving capital, and benefiting from long-term market forces. Unlike a traditional business, property does not inherently require constant operational involvement to perform.

At the same time, property offers flexibility that few other asset classes can match. By increasing management intensity through portfolio expansion, serviced accommodation, or development, property can begin to resemble a business, with greater complexity and the potential for enhanced returns. Crucially, this shift does not change the nature of the asset itself; it changes only how actively it is managed.

This is what makes property such a powerful vehicle for wealth creation. The same asset can deliver steady income and long-term growth or be actively operated to accelerate cash flow and value creation. Understanding this distinction allows investors to choose a level of involvement that aligns with their goals, risk tolerance, and lifestyle, while still benefiting from the enduring strengths of property as an investment.

CHAPTER SUMMARY

Chapter 1 establishes the foundations of property investment by explaining why property is a resilient, demand driven asset, how it differs from running a traditional business, and why knowledge, preparation, and disciplined stewardship are essential for long term success.

KEY POINTS

- Property investment is explained as a durable and widely relied-upon asset, distinct from operating a traditional business.
- Property serves as housing, workplaces, places of worship, centres of trade, and spaces where communities form, giving it enduring strength.
- Owning property is strategic rather than speculative, as it is a foundational asset positioned at the intersection of necessity, resilience, and long-term wealth creation.
- Property investment involves ownership of a property asset to generate returns through rental income, capital appreciation, or both, often with limited day-to-day involvement.
- Successful investors share a commitment to lifelong learning, as property markets evolve constantly. Knowledge directly influences decision-making, negotiation strength, risk management, and ultimately profitability.
- Investors typically fall into three key **Investor Archetypes**: ***Passive Investor*** – low involvement, steady income, long term focus. ***Portfolio Builder*** – medium involvement, structured systems, scalable growth. ***Active Operator*** – high involvement, value creation through active management or development.

Chapter 2 Stewardship: The Essential Framework

"To whom much is given, much will be required." — Luke 12:48, ESV Bible

Property investment is often discussed in terms of numbers: yield, leverage, capital growth, loan-to-value ratios, and tax efficiency. These metrics matter, but on their own they are incomplete. Sustainable wealth, particularly in property, requires a broader framework: stewardship. Before we explore the seven reasons in Build Wealth Through Property, it is essential to situate property and wealth creation within that framework.

Stewardship shifts property investment from short-term profit-seeking to long-term financial stability, resilience, and legacy. Without it, investors may accumulate assets yet undermine their outcomes through excessive risk, poor decision-making, or short-term thinking.

The market offers many examples of investors who acquired multiple properties rapidly, fuelled by leverage and rising prices, but without the discipline or structure required to sustain them. In favourable conditions, their portfolios appeared successful. When interest rates rose, void periods emerged, or refinancing conditions tightened, those same portfolios became liabilities. Forced sales followed, equity was eroded, and years of effort were undone not because property failed, but because stewardship was absent.

This pattern extends beyond property. Sudden wealth without understanding often leads to collapse. The well-documented stories of lottery winners who end up bankrupt, financially distressed, or trapped in destructive habits and addictions serve as a sobering reminder: wealth itself is not the problem; the absence of stewardship is.

Property does not merely amplify returns; it amplifies behaviour. Without stewardship, leverage becomes recklessness, growth becomes excess, and opportunity turns into exposure. Wealth acquired without purpose ceases to be a tool and becomes a burden. It is often said that wealth is a good servant but a poor master.

Stewardship ensures that property serves the investor and the wider society, rather than the investor becoming a servant to their portfolio.

DEFINING STEWARDSHIP IN PROPERTY INVESTMENT

In the context of property, stewardship is the disciplined management of assets, capital, time, and risk to achieve sustainable outcomes and purposeful use of returns. A property investor is not merely an owner but a custodian of buildings, neighbourhoods, tenant relationships, capital, and future value. Properties existed before the current investor and, when managed well, will exist long after.

This perspective reshapes decision-making. Stewardship asks not only 'can this be done?' but also 'should it be done?', and 'at what long-term cost or benefit?'

OWNERSHIP VERSUS CUSTODIANSHIP

People who invest in land and property are commonly referred to as landlords or owners. Yet, in a fundamental sense, no investor creates land. The primary drivers of property value such as land scarcity, population growth, infrastructure development, and the passage of time exist independently of any individual participant in the market.

What investors do control is how responsibly they manage what they acquire and the value they add over time. Buildings deteriorate without care. Neighbourhoods decline when properties are neglected and standards fall. Conversely, well-stewarded property preserves value, attracts consistent demand, and compounds returns over decades, often outliving the investors themselves.

Property rewards those who understand that ownership is, in practice, custodianship. It carries obligations: ongoing maintenance, regulatory compliance, prudent financial management, and ethical treatment of tenants. When these responsibilities are honoured, the benefits extend beyond the individual investor, strengthening communities and creating assets that serve both present needs and future generations.

PURPOSE-DRIVEN INVESTMENT

Property is a powerful tool. As later chapters will explore, it can generate stable income, hedge against inflation, and preserve wealth across generations. These outcomes, however, are not automatic. They depend on alignment between purpose and strategy. Stewardship provides the framework that holds this alignment in place, ensuring that investment decisions are not only profitable, but sustainable.

Some investors pursue wealth with a purely consumerist mindset. They are often hype-driven, swayed by trends, and vulnerable to schemes that promise speed without substance. In such cases, wealth is acquired without direction and quickly dissipated. In contrast, investors who operate with a disciplined, purpose-driven mindset treat income as a tool rather than a trophy. Returns are deployed intentionally whether to transition from salaried employment into greater autonomy, to reinvest and compound toward financial independence, or to support family, community, and charitable causes.

An investor who understands why they invest is less likely to over-leverage, panic during market corrections, or chase speculative returns. Purpose introduces restraint as much as it fuels ambition. It governs risk, moderates emotion, and brings clarity when conditions become uncertain.

Ultimately, property portfolios built with purpose tend to endure. They are not dependent on momentum, market euphoria, or constant expansion. They are shaped by stewardship patient, deliberate, and resilient allowing wealth to be built, preserved, and passed on rather than merely accumulated and consumed.

CLOSING PERSPECTIVE

Property investment is one of the most reliable wealth-building mechanisms available, but only when placed within the framework of stewardship. Stewardship transforms property from a speculative vehicle into a stable platform for financial security, generational wealth, and long-term impact. It aligns ambition with responsibility and growth with endurance.

Money itself is not the ultimate measure of success. It facilitates transactions, but it cannot replace character, trust, or reputation. The true measure of success lies in the impact that wealth has beyond the individual. This truth is powerfully captured by Ugo Bassi, who wrote:

"Measure thy life by loss and not by gain; not by the wine drunk, but by the wine poured forth. For love's strength standeth in love's sacrifice, and he who suffers most has most to give."

CHAPTER SUMMARY

This chapter emphasizes the importance of stewardship in property investment, highlighting the need for disciplined management, long-term financial stability, and alignment between purpose and strategy to ensure sustainable and responsible wealth creation.

KEY POINTS

- Stewardship in property investment shifts the focus from short-term gain to long-term financial stability, resilience, and legacy.
- Accumulating properties without discipline, structure, or proper planning increases exposure to risk and can destabilise an investor's portfolio.
- Property investors act as custodians of buildings, neighbourhoods, tenant relationships, and future value, carrying responsibility beyond simple ownership.
- Purposeful investment ensures that decisions align with long-term goals, creating sustainable and intentional outcomes.
- Property amplifies behaviour; without stewardship, leverage and growth can easily turn into recklessness and financial vulnerability.
- Stewardship preserves long-term impact, ensuring that property serves the investor and the wider community rather than becoming a burden or source of instability.

Chapter 3 Understanding Property Investment Risk

"The biggest risk in property is assuming that property has no risk." — Anonymous

WHY RISK EDUCATION MATTERS

Most people step into property with optimism, convinced that buying bricks and mortar is a guaranteed route to wealth. But investing without understanding risk isn't really investing at all; it is speculation dressed up as strategy.

The 2008 financial crisis demonstrated this brutally. Across the UK, property values fell sharply, and thousands who believed prices could only rise watched their equity evaporate. The crash didn't just expose weak markets; it exposed weak assumptions. Those who understood risk survived. Those who didn't, paid for the lesson. I lived through it and survived. This chapter examines the key risks inherent in property investment and demonstrates how disciplined planning, structure, and decision-making can significantly mitigate those risks. Other risks are also explored within each chapter. While no investment is risk-free, the most common property risks are both foreseeable and manageable.

MARKET RISK

The first major risk is the market itself. It is important to understand that property markets, like all markets, move in cycles. They rise and they fall, and the falls can be deep and prolonged. In the UK, national house prices declined sharply during the downturns of 1989–1992 and again during the 2007–2009 global financial crisis. In the early 1990s, real house prices fell by around one-third from peak to trough, with nominal prices down by roughly 20 per cent before recovery began. During the financial crisis, average UK prices fell by around 15 per cent in 2008–09 and took several years to return to previous peak levels.[6]

Crucially, recovery has never been uniform. Regional house price cycles differ significantly in both depth and duration. After the 2007 downturn, London and the Southeast recovered more quickly, while Northern Ireland and several northern regions experienced much slower rebounds. In Northern Ireland, prices fell by more than 50 per cent from their peak, and by the early 2010s had recovered to only around 63 per cent of their 2007 level, illustrating how severe downturns can leave lasting scars on regional markets.[7]

A more recent example can be seen in Aberdeen. Following the collapse in global oil prices in 2014, the local housing market entered a prolonged period of decline. Prices fell materially from their mid-2010s peak and, unlike many other UK cities, remained well below previous highs for an extended period. Even as house prices across Scotland recovered in nominal terms after the pandemic, Aberdeen

---

[6] Nationwide Building Society (various years) *UK House Price Index: Long-Term Historical Data.* Swindon: Nationwide; Office for National Statistics (ONS) (various years) *UK House Price Index.* London: ONS; Bank of England (1990s; 2008–2009) *Housing market and interest rate statistics.*

[7] Northern Ireland Housing Executive (2011) *Strategic Housing Market Analysis.* Belfast: NIHE; Office for National Statistics (ONS) *UK House Price Index: Northern Ireland.*

continued to underperform, reflecting the impact of local economic dependence on a single dominant industry.[8]

Taken together, these examples show that while property has historically risen over the long term at a national level, it does not do so smoothly or evenly. Prices can fall sharply, remain depressed for many years in certain regions, and recover at very different rates depending on local economic structure, timing, and leverage. The belief that property always goes up, regardless of circumstance, is therefore a comforting simplification rather than a complete truth.

The failures of lenders like Northern Rock and Bradford & Bingley underscored how quickly financial conditions can shift. When confidence drains from the market, the impact spreads: lenders pull back, buyers retreat, and values slump.

Mitigation

Market conditions are shaped by a wide range of economic, demographic, and policy-related factors, and market risk over the life of a property investment is unavoidable and cannot be eliminated. However, the following measures can help mitigate potential disruption:

Avoid Single-Economy Exposure

Property markets that are heavily reliant on a single employer or industry are inherently more vulnerable to prolonged downturns. Aberdeen's historic dependence on oil and gas illustrates how a regional market can suffer when a dominant sector contracts. A similar lesson can be seen in the town of Dagenham in East London, where Ford Motor Company ended passenger car manufacturing at its Dagenham plant in 2002, resulting in significant job losses and a

[8] Office for National Statistics (ONS) *UK House Price Index: Aberdeen City*; Registers of Scotland *UK House Price Index Scotland*; Nationwide Building Society *UK Regional House Price Statistics*.

period of economic adjustment in the surrounding area.[9]

While opportunities exist in every market, a resilient investment strategy should favour locations with diversified employment bases, where no single employer or industry determines demand. Diverse local economies tend to absorb shocks more effectively and recover faster. Where exposure to a single-industry market is unavoidable, risk can be mitigated by diversifying across multiple locations, ensuring that weakness in one area does not undermine the entire portfolio.

Select Entry Level

While market cycles cannot be timed with precision, investors can and should avoid overheated markets. During the property boom in Northern Ireland, I sought to purchase a property in 2006 but was consistently outbid, as demand far outstripped supply. Investors were entering the market from outside the country, demand was significantly outstripping supply, and banks were increasingly willing to lend on properties at prices well above valuation.

In such conditions, discipline matters. Markets characterised by rapid price acceleration, speculative demand, and credit-fuelled growth warrant caution. When price momentum is driven more by easy finance and sentiment than by fundamentals, the margin for error narrows sharply and risk increases.

Recognise Regional Cycles Are Independent

National averages mask local realities. A strategy built on "UK prices always recover" ignores the fact that some regions such as Northern Ireland after 2007 took more than a decade to stabilise and never fully returned to prior peaks in real terms. Investors should assess regional supply, demographics, and economic resilience independently.

---

[9] Ford Motor Company (2002) *Ford ends car production at Dagenham.* Available via Ford Motor Company archives and UK press coverage.

Plan for Extended Recovery Periods

Market risk is not just about falling prices, but about how long capital can remain impaired. Assume that recovery may take many years in certain regions, and structure expectations accordingly. Property is not a mark-to-market asset[10]; capital may be locked in below peak values for long periods.

LEVERAGE RISK

Borrowing is powerful. It can accelerate growth when markets rise, but it also magnifies losses when they fall. For that reason, leverage must be used with discipline and supported by proper stress testing, as discussed further in the chapter on leverage.

Many landlords learned this lesson the hard way because they borrowed excessively and were left exposed when property values fell and interest rates rose. Higher interest rates place strain on the housing market as a whole. First-time buyers and investors alike are discouraged and as such demand weakens, putting a downward pressure on prices. As values declined, some portfolios were pushed into negative equity and at the same time, higher borrowing costs (interest rate) eroded cash flow.

Investors who invested in properties where cash flow was marginal or negative and relied on personal funds to break even were exposed when interest rates increase. The situation was compounded further as selling was no longer a viable option in a depressed market, and refinancing was often unavailable due to over-leverage.

For some, the pressure became severe enough and they ended up with their properties being repossessed. This serves as a clear reminder that while leverage (borrowing) can be a valuable tool, it

---

[10] A *mark-to-market asset* is an asset whose value is regularly re-priced based on current market prices, often daily, reflecting what it could be sold for at that moment rather than its original cost or long-term fundamentals.

is never risk-free and must always be managed with a clear understanding of market cycles, interest-rate risk, and downside exposure.

Mitigation

Interest rates and market conditions are influenced by many variables, and interest rate risk over the life of a mortgage is significant and cannot be eliminated. However, the following measures can help mitigate potential disruption:

Disciplined Use of Leverage

Borrowing should enhance a fundamentally sound investment, not compensate for weak economics. If an asset does not stand on its own merits before debt, leverage will only amplify its weaknesses. Alternatively, investment can be purchased without leverage (borrowing) and that will totally eliminate the risk that leverage poses.

Maintain Conservative Loan-to-Value Ratios

Lower leverage provides a buffer against falling values and protects refinancing options when market conditions tighten. Over-leverage removes flexibility at precisely the moment it is most needed.

Stress-Test Debt

Leverage risk is primarily a debt risk. Investors should assess whether borrowing remains sustainable under higher interest rates, reduced valuations, and restricted lending conditions. If refinancing is required for survival, the structure is fragile.

Keep Enough Equity to Withstand Downturns

Equity acts like a financial safety cushion. When property values fall, properties with healthy equity are better able to absorb the shock without forcing a sale or creating negative equity.

INCOME RISK

A property may appear profitable on paper, but real-world cash flow ultimately reveals the truth. Most landlords will experience void periods, often totalling six to twelve weeks per year. When tenants move out and it takes time to get a new tenant in, or tenants default and the legal process to regain possession can extend for four to six months, during which mortgage payments, insurance, and other costs must still be met.

Income risk is therefore fundamental. For leveraged properties, the inability to service the mortgage places the asset at direct risk of repossession. This is not a theoretical concern. My own experience, discussed in Chapter 12, illustrates how quickly income disruption can transform what appears to be a "safe investment" into a source of significant financial and emotional strain.

Mitigation

Rental income is influenced by tenant behaviour, local demand, and broader economic conditions, and income risk over the life of a property investment is unavoidable. It cannot be eliminated, however, the following measures can help mitigate potential disruption:

Prioritising Certainty Over Yield

While income risk cannot be eliminated entirely, it can be structured and managed. One approach adopted by some landlords is letting to councils, housing associations, or through government-backed schemes. Others use guaranteed rent arrangements, often facilitated by managing agents under contractual agreements.

These structures prioritise income certainty over maximum yield, typically providing rent at below full market levels in exchange for reduced volatility and predictable cash flow. In effect, the investor trades upside for stability. When used deliberately and in the right context, such arrangements can form part of a broader risk-management strategy.

Avoid Reliance on Personal Subsidy

Using personal income to support marginal or negative cash-flowing properties introduces hidden leverage. When personal or external income is disrupted or costs rise, the investment becomes unsustainable.

INTEREST RATE RISK

Interest rates can change the entire economics of a property investment.

For example, between 2022 and 2023, buy-to-let mortgage rates rose sharply, moving from around 3 per cent to approximately 6 per cent in a relatively short period, driven partly by post-pandemic stimulus-induced inflation. For many landlords, myself included, this effectively doubled the cost of borrowing and placed immediate pressure on cash flow. On a £150,000 mortgage, that shift translated into roughly £4,500 per year in additional interest costs, without any corresponding increase in rental income to absorb the impact.

The issue with interest-rate rises is not merely the higher payment, but the speed of adjustment. Mortgage costs reprice quickly, particularly for those on variable rates or expiring fixed-rate deals. Rental income, by contrast, adjusts slowly. It is constrained by tenancy agreements, affordability thresholds, and local market conditions. This creates a timing gap in which costs rise rapidly while income lags.

This period reinforces a central truth of property investment: returns are not driven by price alone. They are shaped just as much by the cost of money, the resilience of cash flow, and the investor's ability to absorb shocks when economic conditions shift.

Mitigation

Interest-rate risk cannot be avoided entirely, but it can be materially reduced through structure and discipline.

Fixing Debt for Longer Periods

Longer fixed-rate mortgages provide payment certainty and protect cash flow during rate spikes. While this may come at a premium, it functions as insurance against volatility during the lifetime of the fixed rate.

Conservative Stress Testing

Properties should be assessed at interest rates well above prevailing levels. If a deal only works at today's rates, it is fragile. A good deal should be able to withstand the shock of rate hike. A margin of safety is essential.

Strong Cash Reserves

Liquidity buffers allow investors to absorb temporary increases in costs without becoming forced sellers or making short-term decisions under pressure.

Rental Headroom at Purchase

Buying below market rent, or in locations with durable tenant demand, creates room for gradual rental adjustments over time, even if income cannot rise immediately.

Interest rates are simply the cost of leveraging (borrowing) and by itself do not destroy property investments overnight. It is the fragile cash flow and indiscipline in borrowing that does.

LIQUIDITY RISK

A defining characteristic of property as an asset class is its illiquidity; it cannot be quickly or easily converted into cash without cost or delay. Even in healthy market conditions, a sale typically takes three to six months to complete. While illiquidity can encourage long-term discipline, it also introduces risk, particularly when capital is required urgently or during market downturns.

In such circumstances, investors may have little choice but to sell at a discount in order to secure a buyer. This is the reality of illiquid assets: timing is not always within your control, and forced sales often crystallise losses that might otherwise have been avoided.

Mitigation

Illiquidity cannot be eliminated, but it can be managed intelligently. The key is to avoid ever becoming a forced seller. Here are the most effective protections:

Maintain Adequate Liquidity Buffers

Holding sufficient cash reserves - typically six to twelve months of expenses and property costs - will provide breathing space during unexpected events. This allows time for markets to recover rather than forcing a distressed sale.

Conservative Use of Leverage

High levels of borrowing amplify illiquidity risk. Sensible loan-to-value ratios reduce pressure during refinancing, interest-rate shocks, or rental voids, lowering the likelihood of needing to sell at the wrong time.

Stress-Test Before You Buy

Investors should model worst-case scenarios: interest-rate rises, prolonged void periods, or reduced rental income. If the asset cannot survive stress without a sale, the structure is fragile.

Match Strategy to Time Horizon

Property is best suited to investors with a long-term outlook. Capital that may be required in the short term should not be tied up in illiquid assets.

Diversification of Income, Not Just Assets

Supplementary income streams outside the property itself reduce reliance on forced disposals to meet financial obligations.

Illiquidity only becomes dangerous when it meets poor planning. The risk is not the asset—it is being forced to sell it.

REGULATORY RISK

Property investing does not take place in a static environment. Regulatory risk arises from changes in government policy, tax treatment, and local authority requirements, all of which can materially affect the viability of an investment.

Over time, governments revise tax rules, councils introduce new licensing schemes, and compliance standards evolve. In the UK, measures such as the restriction of mortgage interest relief under Section 24[11], the tightening of EPC[12] energy efficiency requirements, and the expansion of mandatory and additional licensing regimes have significantly increased both costs and administrative burden for landlords.

As a result, a portfolio that was profitable five years ago may struggle under today's regulatory framework not because the properties themselves have changed, but because the rules governing them have. Regulatory risk therefore operates independently of market performance and must be treated as a core investment risk rather than a peripheral concern.

Mitigation

While regulatory risk cannot be eliminated, it can be managed

---

[11] Section 24 of the Finance (No. 2) Act 2015 restricts individual UK residential landlords from deducting mortgage interest in full when calculating taxable rental profits, replacing this with a basic-rate tax credit set.

[12] Energy Performance Certificate (EPC) is a legally required assessment of a property's energy efficiency in the UK, expressed on a scale from A (most efficient) to G (least efficient). EPCs provide information on a building's energy use, typical energy costs, and recommendations for improving efficiency. For rental properties, minimum EPC standards apply, and properties that do not meet the required threshold may be unlawful to let unless a valid exemption is in place.

through informed and proactive strategy:

Policy awareness: Investors should remain informed about proposed and enacted regulatory changes, particularly in relation to taxation, energy efficiency standards, and local authority licensing. Anticipating change allows time for adjustment rather than reactive decision-making.

Conservative structuring: Using prudent leverage, maintaining adequate cash reserves, and stress-testing investments against higher compliance costs can create resilience when regulations tighten.

Asset selection: Properties that are energy efficient, well-located, and adaptable to changing standards tend to be more resilient to regulatory shifts than marginal assets with limited improvement potential.

Professional advice: Engaging qualified accountants, solicitors, and managing agents ensures regulatory changes are understood correctly and responded to in a compliant and cost-effective manner.

Portfolio flexibility: Avoiding over-concentration in a single regulatory category (for example, heavily licensed HMOs in one local authority) reduces exposure to sudden rule changes.

Regulatory risk does not change the property itself, but it can fundamentally change the economics of owning it.

CHAPTER SUMMARY

This chapter examines the fundamental risks inherent in property investment, demonstrating that while property can be a powerful wealth-building tool, it is not risk-free. It outlines market, leverage, income, interest-rate, liquidity, and regulatory risks, emphasising that disciplined structure, conservative planning, and informed decision-making are essential to preserving capital and ensuring long-term resilience.

KEY POINTS

- Property investment carries inherent risks; assuming otherwise transforms investing into speculation.
- Market cycles are uneven and regionally independent, and prolonged downturns can materially impair capital for years.
- Leverage magnifies both gains and losses; excessive borrowing removes flexibility and increases vulnerability during downturns.
- Cash flow resilience is critical, as income disruption, void periods, or rising interest rates can quickly destabilise over-leveraged portfolios.
- Liquidity risk means property cannot be exited quickly without cost, making cash reserves and long-term planning essential.
- Regulatory changes can materially alter the economics of property ownership, requiring ongoing awareness, prudent structuring, and professional guidance.

Enjoying this book?

I've created a free Property Investor Starter Pack exclusively for readers. It includes helpful tools and spreadsheets that you can use to analyse deals.

Download it free at: BuildWealthThroughProperty.com/start

CHAPTER SUMMARY

[illegible]

Enjoying this book?

[illegible]

Chapter 4 Property: Multiple Pathways to Wealth

"The best investment on earth is earth." — Louis Glickman

The previous chapters established the foundations of property investment and the framework of stewardship and risk that governs how property should be approached responsibly. With those principles in place, this chapter marks a transition from framework to explanation. We now turn to the first of the seven reasons why property investment has consistently endured as a powerful vehicle for building income, resilience, and long-term wealth – Multiple pathways

When most people think about property investment, they imagine a single route: buying a house and renting it out. In reality, property offers a wide range of pathways, each capable of building wealth in different ways and at different speeds. This flexibility is one of the core reasons property remains such a powerful and resilient wealth-building vehicle. Property does not confine investors to one model or strategy. Instead, it opens multiple doors, each leading to a different type of financial outcome.

Before exploring the remaining reasons why property is so effective at building wealth, it is important to recognise this foundational truth: property gives you options. Options are the bedrock of resilience and long-term financial growth. The strength of property lies not only in its stability, tangibility, and ability to generate income, but also in its remarkable versatility.

You can focus on steady rental income, pursue capital growth, specialise in higher-yield strategies, or build a diversified portfolio that evolves as your experience and capital grows. Some investors want reliable monthly cash flow. Others prefer short bursts of profit from buying and selling. Some seek hands-off income, while more seasoned investors combine several routes over time.

In this chapter, we explore the primary pathways through which property builds wealth, demonstrate the breadth of opportunities available, and identify which investor archetypes introduced in the previous chapter are best suited to each opportunity. For the purposes of this book, property investment strategies can be grouped into the following broad pathways:

- Buy-to-Let (Standard Residential Lettings)
- Specialist Residential Rental Strategies
- Residential Trading Strategies
- Property Development
- Commercial Property Investment
- Land Banking

In addition, we briefly consider mixed-use property, care and supported living, and property funds to show how they fit within the wider property landscape.

RESIDENTIAL BUY-TO-LET (SINGLE-LET PROPERTIES)

One of the most familiar and accessible routes into property investment is traditional residential buy-to-let. This involves purchasing a house or apartment and renting it to a single household, whether an individual, couple, or family. The simplicity of this model makes it particularly well suited to the **Passive Investor**, while its reliability has also made it a cornerstone strategy for many **Portfolio Builders**.

The fundamental appeal of single-let property lies in the constant demand for housing. In many cities, chronic housing shortages support stable occupancy and predictable income. These properties are generally straightforward to finance, relatively easy to manage, and more liquid when the time comes to sell. For many investors, residential buy-to-let forms the foundation upon which a broader portfolio is built, either as a long-term passive holding or as the first step toward a more actively managed portfolio.

SPECIALIST RESIDENTIAL RENTAL STRATEGIES

Residential property extends far beyond the standard buy-to-let model. Several specialist strategies exist that can enhance income or target specific tenant groups, depending on an investor's objectives and appetite for involvement.

Houses in Multiple Occupation (HMOs)

Houses in Multiple Occupation represent a more intensive form of residential property investment, typically involving the rental of individual rooms within a single property. This strategy is most commonly associated with the **Portfolio Builder**, though it can also appeal to the **Active Operator** when scale and optimisation are key objectives.

HMOs often generate higher income than single-let properties, reflecting the increased management complexity and regulatory requirements. Demand is driven by affordability pressures, particularly in urban centres with large student populations or transient workforces. While financing, licensing, and compliance are more involved, HMOs reward investors who are willing to implement systems and oversight, making them a natural progression for those moving beyond passive ownership. As such, HMOs are generally unsuitable for the Passive Investor, as they require ongoing compliance management, tenant coordination, and active operational oversight.

Student Accommodation

Student accommodation involves renting property specifically to students, either as shared housing or purpose-built units near educational institutions. This strategy most naturally aligns with the **Portfolio Builder**, though it can also suit the **Active Operator** where scale or specialised management is involved.

Demand for student housing is driven by university enrolment, limited on-campus supply, and affordability pressures in university towns and cities. Income is often structured around academic cycles, with high occupancy during term time and the need for proactive planning around void periods. While management requirements are higher than single-let properties, they are typically more predictable than those of short-term accommodation.

Student accommodation rewards investors who understand local demand, licensing requirements, and tenant dynamics. For Portfolio Builders, it offers enhanced yields through shared occupancy while remaining grounded in long-term residential demand. For Active Operators, particularly those managing multiple units or working with nomination agreements, it can function as a semi-operational model with systems and scale.

Short-Term and Holiday Lets

Serviced accommodation occupies the space between property investment and hospitality. This strategy aligns most closely with the **Active Operator**, as it requires a high degree of operational involvement and day-to-day decision-making.

Income is driven by short-term occupancy, dynamic pricing, and customer experience rather than long-term tenancy agreements. Platforms such as Airbnb and Booking.com introduce both opportunity and volatility, with performance closely tied to location, seasonality, and management quality. While serviced accommodation can produce strong cash flow, it demands disciplined systems, active oversight, and a tolerance for operational complexity, making it less suitable for investors seeking a hands-off approach.

Care and Supported Living

Care and supported living properties are typically leased to specialist operators who provide accommodation for elderly residents or individuals requiring supported housing. These properties are most closely aligned with the Passive Investor and the Portfolio Builder, as they often involve longer lease structures and, in some cases, government-backed or contractually supported income streams.

While this model can offer a high degree of income stability, it also introduces reliance on the operating provider and exposure to regulatory oversight. As such, it is best suited to investors who understand the sector or who work closely with experienced professionals capable of managing operational, contractual, and compliance risks.

DIFFERENCE IN LEGAL RIGHTS BETWEEN SHORT-TERM LETS AND LONGER-TERM RESIDENTIAL TENANCIES.

It is important to note that there is a fundamental difference between Short-term lets and longer-term tenancies. Short-term lets (typically under 12 months and often used for holiday or serviced accommodation) offer greater flexibility to the property owner. Occupiers generally do not have long-term security of tenure, and possession can usually be regained more easily once the agreed period ends.

Long-term residential lettings are different. Once a tenancy is established, tenants benefit from significant legal rights, including protection from eviction except in exceptional circumstances and through formal legal procedures. This materially affects risk, flexibility, and exit strategy particularly if you need to sell the property, as vacant possession may not be immediately available and must be factored into both timing and price.

RESIDENTIAL TRADING STRATEGIES (FLIPS)

While many investors focus on long-term income and capital appreciation, others pursue faster capital gains through residential trading. Commonly referred to as flipping, this strategy aligns most closely with the **Active Operator**, as it involves buying property below market value, adding value through light refurbishment and selling for a profit.

Residential trading can generate significant lump-sum returns over shorter timeframes, but it also carries higher risk. Cost overruns, market shifts, and delays can quickly erode profits. Success in this strategy depends on disciplined acquisition, effective project management, and strict cost control, making it best suited to investors with the time, experience, and risk tolerance to manage active execution.

PROPERTY DEVELOPMENT

Property development involves acquiring property or land and increasing its value through construction, conversion, or substantial refurbishment. This strategy aligns most strongly with the **Active Operator**, as returns are driven less by passive market movement and more by planning, execution, and disciplined delivery.

Development can range from small residential projects to large-scale schemes and typically requires greater capital, deeper expertise, and a higher level of involvement than most buy-to-let strategies. When managed effectively, it offers one of the most powerful pathways for value creation within property, but it also demands a tolerance for complexity and risk. For this reason, development is generally unsuitable for the Passive Investor, as it requires sustained decision-making, hands-on oversight, and active risk management.

At the higher end of development, the activity clearly takes on the characteristics of a business operation. Success depends on coordinating a wide range of professional disciplines, including architects, planners, surveyors, accountants, contractors, and sales agents. The investor becomes responsible for budgeting, timelines, regulatory compliance, financing, and risk management, with outcomes determined primarily by execution rather than ownership alone.

Difference between Flipping and Property Development.

Property flipping and property development are often spoken about interchangeably, yet they describe fundamentally different activities. Flipping is best understood as a trading strategy rather than a development process. The investor purchases a property at a discount, typically due to condition, distress, or mispricing, and seeks to realise a profit through resale within a short time frame. Any works undertaken are primarily focused on improving presentation or marketability, allowing existing value to be revealed rather than materially altered. The profit in a flip is therefore highly sensitive to market conditions, cost control, and timing.

Property development, by contrast, is a value-creation process. It involves changing the underlying characteristics of an asset by altering its structure, use, density, or legal status. This may include extensions, conversions, reconfiguration of layouts, or changes of use that increase the property's functional utility and long-term worth. In development, value is created through planning, design, and execution rather than market momentum alone. While a developed property may ultimately be sold, the sale represents the exit of a development project, not the definition of it. In this sense, flipping describes how an investor exits, whereas development describes where the value originates.

COMMERCIAL PROPERTY INVESTMENT

Commercial property includes assets used by businesses rather than households, such as offices, retail units, warehouses, healthcare facilities, hospitality venues, and mixed-use developments. This strategy most naturally aligns with the **Passive Investor** and the **Portfolio Builder**, particularly where longer lease structures transfer repair and maintenance responsibilities to tenants, resulting in predictable income and reduced day-to-day involvement.

However, commercial property typically requires larger capital commitments, deeper due diligence, including detailed analysis of leases, tenant strength, yield sustainability, and local market conditions, alongside a sound understanding of economic cycles. Void periods can be longer, and tenant demand may be more sensitive to market conditions. For these reasons, commercial property is generally unsuitable for the Active Operator seeking rapid value creation, as returns are driven more by lease structure and market stability than by hands-on operational execution.

Commercial property can, however, suit the **Active Operator** where value is created through redevelopment, refurbishment, or change-of-use, such as converting underutilised office or retail space into alternative commercial or residential uses.

For investors prioritising long-term income and structured risk, commercial property remains a compelling and often hands-off investment option when acquired and managed carefully.

MIXED-USE PROPERTY

Mixed-use property combines residential and commercial elements within a single asset, offering diversified income streams and spreading risk across different tenant types. In the UK, a common example is shop and uppers, where a ground-floor commercial unit, such as a barbershop, pharmacy, or café, generates commercial rent while the upper floors provide residential income. This structure most naturally aligns with the **Portfolio Builder**, who benefits from diversification while retaining an investment-led approach.

From a planning and valuation perspective, mixed-use properties are often assessed primarily on their commercial element, which can influence lending terms, valuation methodology, and exit options. Changes of use, reconfiguration, or intensification of the residential component may require planning consent and careful strategy. For this reason, mixed-use property is generally unsuitable for the Passive Investor, as it demands greater due diligence, structural understanding, and ongoing oversight than straightforward residential investments.

Mixed-use property can, however, suit the **Active Operator** where value is created through redevelopment, reconfiguration, or change-of-use, particularly when underutilised commercial space is repositioned to enhance residential income. As such, mixed-use investments typically sit between residential and commercial strategies and are best understood as a variation of commercial property rather than a standalone investment pathway.

LAND BANKING

Land banking involves purchasing land with the intention of holding it for long-term appreciation, often linked to increased value, future development or planning potential. Because it typically generates no income while held, this strategy aligns most closely with the **Active Operator** and experienced **Portfolio Builders** who have sufficient capital, patience, and the ability to manage extended time horizons.

Returns depend heavily on planning outcomes, infrastructure investment, and demographic trends rather than rental income. As a result, land banking suits investors with a high tolerance for uncertainty and a disciplined approach to due diligence. For this reason, land banking is generally unsuitable for the Passive Investor, as it offers no immediate cash flow and requires long-term capital commitment with limited visibility on outcomes.

When executed successfully, land banking can deliver substantial gains, but it demands rigorous planning analysis, patience, and a long-term strategic mindset. Because land is a finite resource, land banking can raise ethical questions around intent. The moral challenge is not ownership itself, but purpose. When land is held purely to profit from scarcity, it raises concerns around housing access, affordability, and community wellbeing. When land is held as part of a responsible, long-term development strategy, it can instead reflect stewardship rather than exploitation.

PROPERTY FUNDS AND REITS (A BRIEF CONTRAST)

Property funds and Real Estate Investment Trusts (REITs) provide indirect exposure to property through pooled investment vehicles. This approach aligns most closely with the **Passive Investor**, particularly those who prioritise liquidity, diversification, and minimal involvement over direct control.

While funds and REITs can play a role within a broader investment portfolio, they remove the investor from direct ownership and limit the ability to influence outcomes through strategy, structure, or execution. For this reason, they are generally unsuitable for the Portfolio Builder and the Active Operator, whose approaches rely on direct control, asset-level decision-making, and active value creation.

This book focuses on direct property ownership, where investors retain the ability to shape performance and outcomes. Property funds and REITs are included here for completeness, but they sit outside the core investment approach explored in this book.

CONCLUSION: ONE ASSET CLASS, MANY PATHS

The first reason property is such a powerful driver of wealth is its versatility. Few asset classes offer so many complementary routes to financial success. Whether your objective is steady income, accelerated capital growth, long-term security, or diversification, property provides pathways that can be aligned with your ambitions.

You are not confined to a single model or locked into one strategy. Property allows you to adapt, combine approaches, and scale as your circumstances evolve. This flexibility is the first reason explored. It is also why property remains central to wealth creation for millions because options create resilience, and resilience reduces the risk of failure.

Recognising these pathways is only the beginning. Versatility explains how property works; income explains why it endures. This brings us to the second reason property supports long-term success: its ability to generate predictable, repeatable income, income that continues whether you are working or not and forms the foundation of financial stability and long-term security.

CHAPTER SUMMARY

This chapter explores the multiple pathways to wealth through property investment, highlighting its flexibility and resilience, and detailing various strategies such as buy-to-let, specialist residential rentals, property development, and commercial property investment

KEY POINTS

- Property offers multiple wealth-building pathways, each providing different routes to income, growth, or diversification.
- Residential buy-to-let provides steady, long-term rental income and is one of the simplest and most accessible entry points into property investment.
- Specialist residential strategies—such as HMOs, student accommodation, serviced accommodation, and supported living—offer higher income potential but often require greater involvement and management.
- Residential trading strategies (flips) generate short-term profits through buying, improving, and selling property.
- Property development creates value through construction, conversion, or major refurbishment, offering high potential returns with higher complexity and risk.
- Commercial property provides longer leases, predictable income, and opportunities for diversification across business sectors.
- Mixed-use property combines residential and commercial elements, creating multiple income streams within a single asset.
- Land banking focuses on long-term value appreciation driven by planning potential, infrastructure, and demographic trends.
- Indirect options such as property funds and REITs provide exposure to real estate without direct ownership or operational responsibility.
- Property's versatility enables investors to choose strategies that match their goals, risk tolerance, experience, and desired level of involvement.

Chapter 5
Property: A Source of Income

"Do not depend on a single income. Make investment to create a second source." — Warren Buffett

In this chapter, we examine one of the primary purposes of any investment: its ability to generate income and deliver a return. We explore how property produces cash flow and how investors can make informed decisions by understanding the income a property generates relative to its value.

UNDERSTANDING RENTAL INCOME

Rental income is the most straightforward and widely understood form of income generated by property. It refers to the money received in exchange for allowing others to occupy and use a property. For many investors, rental income provides steady cash flow that supports financial stability while other benefits, such as capital growth, compound over time.

Like many people, rental income was what got me excited about property, particularly the ability to earn income with limited day-to-day involvement. Even with higher interest rates at the time, my first apartment generated positive cash flow, and I was more than happy to receive income without actively working for it. At that stage, I had little understanding of what it truly meant to be a landlord. I was simply excited to own a property and to call myself one.

Over time, I learned about service charges, maintenance responsibilities, and the obligation to declare rental income and pay tax on it. Like many new investors, my education came through experience.

Rental income remains one of the core pillars of property investing because it delivers consistent cash flow over time. However, passive does not mean effort-free. Even the most hands-off investments require sensible oversight. Properties must be maintained, rents collected, and legal responsibilities met. When managed correctly, rental income becomes one of the most reliable and rewarding financial benefits property offers.

DIFFERENT TYPES OF RENTAL INCOME

Rental income can arise from various property types and arrangements.

Residential rentals typically involve houses, apartments, or HMOs leased to individuals or families. These agreements are commonly structured as fixed-term tenancies, often for twelve months, which may subsequently transition into periodic arrangements or be renewed for longer terms.

Commercial rentals, by contrast, involve leasing property for business use, such as offices, retail units, or warehouses. Commercial leases are typically longer, often spanning five to ten years or more, providing greater income predictability over time.

Short-term rentals represent another growing category. These involve letting properties for brief periods, ranging from days to several months. Platforms such as Airbnb and Booking.com have expanded access to this model, catering to tourists, travelling professionals, and those seeking temporary accommodation. While short-term rentals can command higher nightly rates, they require more active management and can be subject to seasonal fluctuations.

Investors can enhance rental income by staying attuned to market trends, upgrading properties to attract higher-quality tenants, and responding to shifts in demand, such as remote working patterns, population growth, student demand, and urbanisation.

FINDING TENANTS

For any property investor, location is a critical determinant of success. Thorough due diligence such as analysing local rental demand, employment drivers, transport links, amenities, and historical rental performance is essential to ensure investment in areas with strong existing demand and clear potential for sustained demand in the future. Properties that are well maintained, competitively priced, and appropriately presented for the rental market are far more likely to attract and retain tenants.

One of the most straightforward ways to secure tenants is to register the property with a reputable local estate agent. For a fee, agents can market the property and, if required, manage it on the investor's behalf. Further details on the services typically provided by estate agents is covered in Chapter 11.

Some investors prefer a more hands-on approach and choose to market and manage their properties independently. In such cases, landlords must take responsibility for sourcing tenants through channels such as online platforms, including Facebook Marketplace or Gumtree. While this approach can reduce costs, it also requires the landlord to manage tenant referencing, compliance checks, and deposit protection independently, responsibilities that would otherwise be handled by an estate agent.

SETTING RENT

Setting the right rent is an important part of the overall investment jigsaw. The rent you charge affects vacancy periods, cash flow, tenant quality, and, consequently, your overall stress levels. You want to avoid both under-renting and pricing yourself out of the market. The core principle is simple: aim for a price that is competitive in the local market while still covering your costs and leaving room for profit. If you price too high, your property will remain vacant for longer, resulting in a loss of income. If you price too low, you leave money on the table and may attract tenants who are more maintenance heavy.

Well before purchasing an investment property for rental purposes, it is essential to research the likely rental income. This is done by reviewing comparable properties on property websites and consulting local estate agents, considering current market conditions and prevailing rents in the area.

CHALLENGES, RISKS, AND HOW TO NAVIGATE THEM

Property investment offers compelling opportunities, but it is not without challenges. The objective is not to eliminate risk entirely, but to understand it and manage it intelligently.

Market Volatility

Market volatility is often the first concern raised by investors. Property values can fluctuate in response to economic conditions, interest rates, and local factors such as infrastructure development or changes in desirability. In my experience, properties acquired in strong locations tend to perform far more resiliently through market cycles. Rental income has historically demonstrated durability over time[13].

Rising Costs and Cash Flow Pressure

Just as cash is king, so also is cash flow for a property investor. Rising operating and management costs can quietly erode cash flow, making your investment to perform poorly. Maintenance, management fees, insurance, and compliance cost all impact net returns. Cost control is just as important as headline rental figures when assessing performance.

Void Periods and Vacancy Risk

Vacancies are an unavoidable reality that investors must plan for. An unoccupied property generates no income while expenses continue. Competitive pricing, proactive management, and effective marketing are essential defences against prolonged voids. A capable managing agent can significantly improve outcomes through strong tenant screening, responsive maintenance, and consistent communication.

Tenant Risk

Tenant quality directly affects both income stability (cash flow) and the condition of a property. I learned this through experience. Early in my investing journey, I assumed that securing a tenant meant the hard work was done. I was wrong.

I have dealt with rent arrears, property damage, and the stress that accompanies a failing tenancy. In the UK, eviction is slow, expensive, and heavily regulated. Obtaining a County Court Judgement (CCJ) is a lengthy process and is not a silver bullet when dealing with a bad tenant. It is one thing to secure a judgment, and

---

[13] According to the UK Office for National Statistics' Price Index of Private Rents, average private rents in the UK have demonstrated steady long-term growth across the last decade, rising substantially from the mid-2010s to 2025 even through economic fluctuations.

quite another to enforce it. A CCJ[14] confirms that money is owed, but it does not compel payment. Enforcement is a separate step, requiring additional time and cost, and in many cases the debt is ultimately unrecoverable. While tenant protections are necessary, they can leave landlords carrying months of financial exposure while mortgage payments, insurance, and maintenance costs continue.

The greatest cost for me, with my experience with bad tenants, is not just financial, but distraction. Time that should have been better spent was consumed by managing problems that could have been avoided. That experience taught me a lasting lesson: poor tenant selection is not a minor risk; it can undermine an otherwise sound investment.

As a result, I became far more disciplined. Thorough reference checks, affordability assessments, clear tenancy agreements, and management via a reputable estate agent became invaluable. Tenant selection is a very important decision for investors. Done well, it protects income, preserves assets, and provides stability and prevents stress. Done poorly, it can unravel everything.

HANDLING NON-PAYING TENANTS AND DIFFICULT SCENARIOS

Here is some advice on how to handle some difficult issues around tenant management.

Non-Paying Tenants

Rent arrears are among the most common and financially draining problems landlords face. When rental income stops, expenses do

[14] County Court Judgment (CCJ): A CCJ is a civil court order issued in England, Wales, and Northern Ireland confirming that a monetary debt is legally owed by a defendant to a claimant. While it establishes legal liability, it does not compel payment. Enforcement requires separate legal action and is subject to procedural, financial, and practical limitations (HM Courts & Tribunals Service, n.d.).

not. Mortgage payments, insurance, and maintenance costs continue regardless of tenant performance.

Early intervention is critical. Clear communication, prompt arrears letters, and structured repayment plans can sometimes resolve issues before they escalate. However, landlords must also recognise when engagement has broken down and take decisive action. Delayed responses often increase losses.

As noted in my personal experience, sound tenant referencing and affordability checks are crucial. In addition, you must plan for it by maintaining adequate financial buffers.

Eviction Processes and Costs (UK Context)

Eviction in the UK is **slow, regulated, and costly**. Whether pursuing a Section 8[15] route for rent arrears or relying on possession through notice procedures, timelines frequently extend for several months.

Costs can include:

- Legal and court fees
- Solicitor costs
- Lost rental income during proceedings
- Additional maintenance or security expenses

Even when possession is granted, recovery of unpaid rent is not guaranteed. This reality reinforces the importance of conservative cash-flow planning and avoiding over-leverage.

Eviction should always be a last resort, but landlords must understand the process fully before problems arise.

---

[15] In England and Wales, landlords may seek fault-based possession under Section 8 of the Housing Act 1988, where statutory grounds such as rent arrears or breach of tenancy conditions are met. In Northern Ireland, possession proceedings are governed by the Private Tenancies (Northern Ireland) Order 2006, which provides for Notice to Quit and court action where required. In Scotland, residential tenancies are regulated under the Private Housing (Tenancies) (Scotland) Act 2016, with eviction grounds determined by the First-tier Tribunal for Scotland (Housing and Property Chamber). Across all jurisdictions, eviction is highly regulated, time-consuming, and may involve significant legal costs and loss of rental income.

Difficult Tenant Scenarios

Beyond non-payment, landlords may encounter tenants who:

- Damage the property
- Refuse access for inspections or repairs
- Breach tenancy agreements
- Create nuisance issues affecting neighbours
- Sublet without permission

These situations can be emotionally taxing as well as financially damaging. Professional property management can provide a valuable buffer, ensuring issues are documented, handled lawfully, and escalated appropriately.

A disciplined, unemotional approach is essential. Property investment is a business, and difficult situations must be managed within legal and contractual boundaries.

Property Damage and Wear-and-Tear

Not all damage is accidental or fair wear-and-tear. Landlords should be prepared for scenarios including:

- Broken fixtures and fittings
- Damaged flooring or doors
- Neglected maintenance leading to larger repairs
- Deliberate vandalism in rare but costly cases

Detailed inventories, photographic evidence (so tenants can't claim that the damage was already there), and regular inspections are critical in protecting a landlord's position. Deposits may cover minor issues, but they rarely compensate fully for extensive damage or prolonged vacancy.

This reinforces the importance of contingency funds and realistic assumptions when forecasting returns. These challenges do not negate the value of property as an investment. Investors who plan conservatively, understand their legal obligations, and accept that setbacks are part of the journey are far better positioned to succeed over the long term.

Property does not fail because problems arise. It fails when problems are ignored, misunderstood, or underestimated.

Maintenance and Repairs

Maintenance and repairs are inevitable. Rather than viewing them as unexpected setbacks, experienced investors treat these costs as predictable components of ownership. Regularly setting aside funds and factoring maintenance into cash-flow projections allows issues to be addressed without unnecessary financial strain.

Management Quality

Management quality plays a critical role in investment performance. Poor management can result in tenant disputes, missed payments, and compliance failures. While professional management reduces risk, it does not remove the need for oversight. Investors should clearly understand service levels, fees, and contractual terms before committing.

Regulatory and Legal Compliance

Regulatory and legal requirements demand ongoing attention. Licensing, safety standards, tenancy regulations, and tax obligations vary by location. Failure to comply can result in fines, enforcement action, or legal exposure. Staying informed and working with qualified professionals provides essential protection. I remember a conversation with my estate agent about getting rid of his services and managing my property myself because I wanted to squeeze a bit more for cash flow. A lecture from him regarding the ever-changing regulatory and compliance law changed my decision, as I personally didn't have the time to keep on top of it all.

Environmental Risk

Environmental considerations should not be overlooked. Flood risk, pollution, and other environmental factors can affect property value, financing, and insurability. Thorough due diligence such as reviewing flood-risk maps, environmental reports, planning history, and lender requirements, together with appropriate insurance are vital safeguards.

Local Supply and Demand Dynamics

Local supply and demand dynamics are equally important. Areas can decline rapidly when key employers or institutions relocate. In Belfast, for example, when Ulster University moved its campus from the outskirts of the city to the city centre, rental demand and supporting businesses declined sharply in the former location, while demand surged around the new campus. Understanding what drives a local economy is essential before committing capital.

A REAL-LIFE LESSON: WHEN INCOME ASSUMPTIONS FAIL

Earlier in my property journey, I experienced what felt like a quick win through an off plan[16] investment. The deal went smoothly, the numbers worked, and the outcome was positive. That early success led me to believe, incorrectly, that off-plan investing followed a reliable and repeatable formula.

Encouraged by that experience, my wife and I invested in another off-plan development in a different part of the city. I negotiated a discount and initially agreed to purchase three apartments, eventually completing on two. On paper, the decision appeared sound. In reality, almost everything that could go wrong did.

By the time the properties were completed, I expected a clear uplift in value. Instead, the market had softened, and there was no meaningful capital growth. The area was not as up-and-coming as I

[16] Off-plan investment refers to the purchase of a property before construction is completed, and in many cases before construction has commenced, based on architectural plans, specifications, and projected timelines. Investors typically secure the property at an early stage—often at a discounted price—with the expectation of capital appreciation by completion. Off-plan investments carry specific risks, including construction delays, specification changes, market fluctuations, and developer insolvency.

was led to believe, and I had not done enough due diligence—particularly around local market fundamentals such as demand, infrastructure, and job creation that would support the area's desirability, as well as timing and independent verification rather than reliance on developer-led projections. Selling was no longer attractive, so we chose to rent the apartments. Securing tenants took longer than anticipated, and we had to reduce the asking rent to generate interest. Even then, rental income fell short of projections, leaving us to subsidise the mortgage payments.

Once tenants were in place, further challenges emerged. Despite full tenant referencing, one tenant later defaulted and fell into arrears. Recovering the outstanding rent required court action. While the process eventually worked in our favour, it was slow, stressful, and costly.

Looking back, the core mistake was not the concept, but the assumptions. I relied too heavily on optimistic expectations around capital appreciation and rental performance. I failed to stress-test the numbers against less favourable scenarios, such as slower demand, reduced rents, or extended voids. The margin for error was far thinner than I had appreciated.

We eventually exited and sold both apartments at a loss. It was a painful experience, but one of the most instructive lessons of my investment journey.

Key takeaway:

Income must be assessed conservatively. Lasting success in property comes from disciplined analysis, realistic assumptions, and preparing for downside risk, not just what looks good on paper. Also note that past performance on a particular deal does not equate to same performance on another deal. Deals are unique. Despite these challenges, property remains one of the most durable wealth-building vehicles available. With preparation, realistic expectations, and professional support, risks become manageable rather than intimidating.

Understanding risk is essential, but awareness alone is not enough. To manage risk effectively, investors must be able to measure performance. This is where the numbers matter.

UNDERSTANDING RENTAL YIELD

Rental yield is one of the most important metrics in property investment. It measures the income a property generates relative to its value and allows investors to compare opportunities objectively.

There are two primary types of rental yield: gross yield and net yield. Gross yield considers income before expenses, while net yield reflects the true return after costs such as maintenance, insurance, management fees, taxes, and allowances for vacancies.

How Gross Rental Yield Is Calculated

Gross rental yield indicates how much income a property produces relative to its value before expenses.

Example:

If a property is worth £250,000 and generates £20,000 in annual rent:

- £20,000 ÷ £250,000 = 0.08
- Gross rental yield = **8%**

Gross yield is useful for quick comparisons but does not reflect true profitability.

How Net Rental Yield Is Calculated

Net rental yield provides a more accurate picture of a property's performance by accounting for operating costs.

Formula:

(Annual Rent – Annual Expenses) ÷ Property Value × 100

Example:

If a property costs £300,000, generates £25,000 in rent, and incurs £7,000 in annual expenses:

- Net income = £18,000
- Net rental yield = **6%**

Net yield offers a realistic assessment of cash flow and investment quality.

CONCLUSION

Rental income is one of the most immediate and tangible benefits of property investment. Yield provides a practical framework for assessing whether a property is working effectively, but income alone should never be considered in isolation. Location, property type, management quality, and long-term growth prospects all play important roles.

While rental income forms the foundation of many successful portfolios, it is only part of the picture. Property's ability to generate income becomes even more powerful when combined with leverage. The capacity to control high-value assets using relatively modest amounts of personal capital is one of property's greatest advantages.

In the next chapter, we explore leverage in detail and examine how it can accelerate wealth creation when used responsibly and strategically.

CHAPTER SUMMARY

The chapter explains how rental income provides steady cash flow and financial stability, highlights different types of rental income, and emphasizes the importance of managing risks and understanding rental yield for successful property investment.

KEY POINTS

- Rental income is a primary source of revenue in property investment, providing steady cash flow that supports financial stability while capital growth accumulates over time.
- Rental income can be generated through several property types, including residential lettings, commercial leases, and short term or holiday rentals.
- Attracting and retaining tenants depends heavily on location, property condition, competitive pricing, and presenting the property appropriately for the rental market.
- Property investment involves risks such as vacancies, rising costs, market changes, and tenant issues; the goal is to understand these risks and manage them effectively rather than attempt to eliminate them.
- Rental yield measures the income a property produces relative to its value and serves as a key metric for objectively comparing investment opportunities.

Chapter 6 Property: The Power of Leverage

Controlling more with less.

What if you could control a property worth four times the amount of cash you have today and still benefit fully from its income and growth? That is the power of leverage.

In property investment, leverage is one of the most powerful tools available. It refers to the strategic use of borrowed money often described as "other people's money" to acquire property and amplify results. When used responsibly, leverage allows investors to control larger assets, accelerate portfolio growth, and compress the time required to build wealth.

GOOD DEBT VS BAD DEBT

Conventional wisdom often warns against borrowing, encouraging people to live within their means. While this advice is sensible in many areas of life, it overlooks an important distinction: not all debt is the same.

Consumer debt is borrowing used for consumption, such as credit cards, personal loans, holidays, overdrafts, or car finance. These liabilities typically fund depreciating assets or short-term experiences, generate no income, and weaken a person's financial position over time. And yes, as much as possible, I'm on the side of conventional wisdom, do not borrow to spend on liabilities.

Investment debt, by contrast, is borrowing used to acquire assets that can produce income or grow in value. A mortgage used to purchase a rental property is investment debt. When structured correctly, it can strengthen financial position by generating cash flow and long-term appreciation.

Borrowing to invest may sound risky, but in property it is both common and practical. Property is a tangible, income-producing asset that lenders understand and trust. This combination of security and cash flow makes property one of the most leverage-friendly investments available.

UNDERSTANDING HOW LEVERAGE WORKS

To appreciate the real impact of leverage, consider the difference between investing with cash alone and investing with borrowed funds.

Assume you have £50,000 available to invest in property. We will compare two approaches using the same starting capital, taking into account both rental income and capital appreciation.

Leverage in Action: One Property vs Four

Option 1: Buying One Property Outright (No Leverage)

A single property is purchased outright for £50,000[17].

- Monthly rent: £500 (£6,000 per year)

[17] The figures used in this chapter are illustrative only and are intended to demonstrate the principles of leverage. They are simplified examples and do not represent actual transactions or investment outcomes.

- Operating costs: £150 per month (£1,800 per year), reflecting typical ongoing expenses including maintenance, management fee, insurance, and day-to-day running costs.

Net rental income: £4,200 per year

Assuming modest capital growth of 5 per cent, the property increases in value by £2,500 in the first year.

Total annual benefit (without leverage):

- £4,200 from rental income
- £2,500 from capital growth

Total: £6,700 on a £50,000 investment

Option 2: Using Leverage to Buy Four Properties

Instead of purchasing one property outright, the same £50,000 is used as deposits. By placing 25 per cent (£12,500) on each property, four properties valued at £50,000 each are acquired.

- Total property value controlled: £200,000
- Mortgage per property: £37,500

Each property generates £500 per month in rent.

Rental income across four properties:

- £2,000 per month
- £24,000 per year

Annual costs:

- Mortgage interest (4% interest-only): £6,000
- Operating costs (£150 per property per month): £7,200

Total annual costs: £13,200

Net rental income: £10,800 per year

Assuming the same 5 per cent capital growth, the £200,000 portfolio increases in value by £10,000 in the first year.

Total annual benefit (with leverage):

- £10,800 from rental income
- £10,000 from capital growth

Total: £20,800 using the same £50,000 of initial capital

PUTTING LEVERAGE INTO PERSPECTIVE

Using identical starting capital, buying one property outright produces £6,700 in annual benefit, while using leverage generates £20,800. Leverage more than triples the outcome by multiplying both income and growth in direct proportion to the value of assets controlled.

The lender provides part of the purchase price, yet the investor retains the full benefit of appreciation and the majority of the cash flow. This is why leverage is such a powerful accelerator in property investment.

One way to understand this is to ask a simple question: which would you rather have—one apple tree you own outright, or four apple trees acquired using borrowed money, all producing fruit immediately, with the debt structured to be paid down over time, say within fifteen years? In the first case, after fifteen years, you own one apple tree; in the second, you own four.

This is the essence of leverage. The goal is not debt for its own sake, but the disciplined use of borrowing to accelerate access to productive assets. When applied with structure, affordability, and a clear plan, leverage becomes one of the reasons property investments when approached correctly dramatically reduces the risk of failure.

However, leverage amplifies outcomes in both directions. Used recklessly, it magnifies losses. Used wisely, it transforms modest capital into a scalable wealth-building engine.

NEGATIVE EQUITY

Negative equity occurs when a property's value falls below its outstanding mortgage. In rising markets, this risk is often ignored, yet it is during downturns that leverage exposes its danger. An investor forced to sell in negative equity may crystallise losses even when the property itself remains sound. Those able to hold on, however, often see well-located assets recover as market conditions improve.

The critical point is this: negative equity only becomes fatal when liquidity fails. Periods of excessive capital chasing limited stock tend to inflate prices and invite correction, as seen across the UK during the 2008 financial crisis. Investors dependent on capital growth and thin margins are therefore most vulnerable. By contrast, those using adequate deposits, sustainable loan-to-value ratios, and resilient rental income are far better positioned to withstand market cycles.

REFINANCING

Refinancing is the process of replacing an existing mortgage with a new one, usually to reflect changes in a property's value, debt position, or to take advantage of low interest rate. In property investment, refinancing is most often used after a period of ownership in which capital growth, rental stabilisation, or value-adding works have improved the underlying asset. By reassessing the property against its updated value, investors may be able to release equity, reduce borrowing costs, or restructure debt through a remortgage in a way that better aligns with their long-term strategy.

Used wisely, refinancing can be a powerful tool for portfolio growth and risk management. Releasing equity allows capital to be recycled into new opportunities without selling existing assets. However, refinancing should always be approached with discipline. It increases exposure to debt and interest rate risk, and extracting equity purely for consumption rather than reinvestment can weaken a portfolio over time. As with leverage itself, refinancing is most effective when it serves a clear purpose and supports the original investment objective rather than undermining it. In the section below, refinancing will be illustrated through an example to highlight both its power and the risks that can arise if circumstances change, particularly in relation to interest rates.

Numerical Illustration: Refinancing in Practice

An investor purchases a property for £150,000 with a 75 per cent mortgage (£112,500) and a 25 per cent deposit (£37,500). Over time, rental income stabilises and modest improvements are made. Several years later, the property is revalued at £200,000.

At the original 75 per cent loan-to-value, the property can now support borrowing of up to £150,000. After repaying the existing mortgage balance of £112,500, the investor is able to release approximately £37,500 in equity. This capital can then be recycled into another investment, while the original property is retained and continues to generate income.

This example illustrates how refinancing can convert unrealised capital growth into deployable capital. When used deliberately and within prudent loan-to-value limits, refinancing allows investors to expand portfolios without selling assets, while maintaining long-term ownership and income generation.

MANAGING RISK IN A LEVERAGED PORTFOLIO

Effective use of leverage requires discipline. Investors must monitor loan-to-value ratios[18], stress-test cash flow[19] against interest-rate

---

[18] Loan-to-Value Ratio (LTV) is a measure lenders use to assess risk. It compares how much you are borrowing to the value of the asset you are buying. It is the percentage of a property's value that is financed with a loan.
How it is calculated LTV = (Loan Amount ÷ Property Value) × 100

[19] Stress-testing cash flow: assessing whether rental income can still cover mortgage and operating costs if interest rates rise above current levels.

changes and maintain sufficient reserves.

Over-leveraging can trap investors by removing margin for error and flexibility. High levels of debt increase sensitivity to interest-rate changes, place constant pressure on cash flow, and limit refinancing or exit options if market conditions shift. In a downturn, falling values can push highly leveraged assets into negative equity, restricting choice and forcing reactive decisions. Rather than accelerating progress, excessive leverage can lock investors into underperforming positions and undermine long-term strategy. Prudent investors balance growth ambitions with resilience, ensuring leverage enhances opportunity rather than undermines stability.

Leverage is not merely an acquisition tool. It is a lifecycle strategy that, when used thoughtfully, allows investors to grow, manage, and preserve wealth over time.

Stress-Test Variation: Higher Interest Rates

Using the same example, assume the refinanced mortgage of £150,000 is subject to an interest rate increase from 3 per cent to 6 per cent. At 3 per cent, the annual interest cost would be approximately £4,500. At 6 per cent, this rises to £9,000 per year.

This doubling of interest costs materially reduces net cash flow and demonstrates why refinancing decisions should not be made solely on headline equity release. A prudent investor would assess whether the property can comfortably service the higher debt under less favourable conditions, allowing for voids, maintenance, and rising operating costs.

This stress-test reinforces a central principle of disciplined leverage: equity should only be released where the underlying income can withstand higher interest rates without compromising the stability of the investment or the wider portfolio.

The 2008 Financial Crisis: A Lesson in Excess and Discipline

The global financial crisis of 2008 exposed the consequences of undisciplined leverage. Investors and institutions alike relied on rising prices, easy credit, and constant refinancing. When values fell and credit tightened, highly leveraged portfolios collapsed—not because property stopped being valuable, but because cash flow and capital structure were insufficient.

Those who survived were not the most aggressive, but the most conservative. Investors with manageable leverage, stable income, and the ability to hold through the downturn preserved their assets and, in many cases, emerged stronger.

WHY PROPERTY ATTRACTS LEVERAGE

Property attracts lending from banks and other creditors because it is tangible, income-producing, and relatively stable. Unlike many financial assets, property generates rent, providing a built-in mechanism for loan repayment. This reassures lenders and makes financing more accessible.

For investors, this availability of credit means that modest savings can unlock control over high-value assets. When managed correctly, leverage turns property from a slow-building investment into a powerful engine for growth.

Common forms of leverage include traditional mortgages, equity release, and lines of credit. Each has advantages and risks depending on the investor's goals, experience, and financial structure.

Bridging Finance and the Hidden Risk of Time

Bridging loans are a type of leverage that occupy a specific and legitimate place within property investment, particularly for acquisitions requiring speed, refurbishment, or resolution of short-term constraints. They are commonly used by active investors and developers to secure opportunities that conventional mortgage finance cannot accommodate. However, bridging finance introduces a distinct category of leverage risk, driven less by market movement and more by time, cost, and penalty exposure.

Unlike traditional mortgages, bridging loans typically carry high monthly interest rates, arrangement fees, and strict exit assumptions. Interest is often rolled up, meaning it compounds throughout the term and becomes payable on exit rather than monthly. While this structure can ease short-term cash flow, it also obscures the true cost of borrowing. When projects overrun, planning is delayed, or sales take longer than expected, extension fees, default interest, and exit penalties can escalate rapidly. In such circumstances, time itself becomes the primary enemy of the investor.

The critical danger with bridging finance is not its use, but its misuse. A bridge should only be entered with a clearly defined, realistic, and controllable exit strategy, supported by conservative timelines and contingency funding. Where the exit depends on optimistic assumptions such as rapid refinancing, rising values, or perfect execution, the bridge ceases to be a tool and becomes a liability. Bridging finance rewards precision and discipline; without them, it can turn leverage into a mechanism of forced loss rather than accelerated gain.

Example:

An investor takes a £200,000 bridging loan at 1.1% per month, with rolled-up interest and an intended term of 9 months.

Stage 1: Expected Outcome (No Delay)

Monthly interest:

£200,000 × 1.1% = **£2,200**

Interest over 9 months:

£2,200 × 9 = **£19,800**

Arrangement fee (2% of loan):

£200,000 × 2% = **£4,000**

Total finance cost at 9 months:

£19,800 + £4,000 = **£23,800**

Total repayment at planned exit:

£200,000 + £23,800 = **£223,800**

At this stage, the project may be viable with the cost of borrowing controllable.

Stage 2: Delayed Exit (15 Months)

Interest over 15 months:

£2,200 × 15 = **£33,000**

Additional interest caused by delay:

£33,000 – £19,800 = **£13,200**

Extension fee: £3,000

Total finance cost after delay:

£33,000 + £4,000 + £3,000 = **£40,000**

Total repayment at delayed exit:

£200,000 + £40,000 = **£240,000**

Stage 3: Default Interest Scenario (Penalty Triggered)

If the loan exceeds the agreed term without formal extension and **default interest of 3% per month** applies for **2 months**:

Default interest per month:

£200,000 × 3% = **£6,000**

Default interest for 2 months:

£6,000 × 2 = **£12,000**

Revised total finance cost:

£40,000 + £12,000 = **£52,000**

Revised total repayment:

£200,000 + £52,000 = **£252,000**

With bridging finance, the original cost may be manageable, but delay converts time into compounding expense and penalties into permanent loss.

LEVERAGE AND EXIT STRATEGY

Leverage influences not only how property is acquired, but also how it is exited. Every investor should begin with the end in mind.

The most common exit strategies include selling, refinancing, holding for long-term income, or transferring assets as part of a legacy plan. Each option carries different implications for cash flow, tax, and risk.

Selling crystallises gains but ends future income and growth. Refinancing allows investors to release equity without selling, often enabling further investment while retaining ownership. Holding builds long-term income and appreciation, while legacy planning focuses on preservation and intergenerational transfer.

Exit decisions must account for mortgage terms, early repayment charges, capital gains tax, and transaction costs. Ignoring these factors can quietly erode returns and turn strong investments into disappointing outcomes.

CONCLUSION: LEVERAGE, DISCIPLINE, AND ENDURING VALUE

Leverage is one of the most transformative concepts in property investment. It enables investors to achieve far more than cash alone, compressing time and expanding opportunity. Used wisely, it allows ordinary capital to control extraordinary assets. Yet its effectiveness depends not on borrowing itself, but on discipline, structure, and strategy.

Mastering leverage means understanding risk, credit, and timing. It requires the ability to balance ambition with restraint, and growth with sustainability. When applied responsibly, leverage becomes a bridge between where an investor is today and where they aim to be tomorrow. When misused, however, it can magnify errors just as easily as it magnifies gains.

This is why patience matters as much as mathematics.

The ancient story of the golden goose captures this principle perfectly. The goose produced one golden egg each day quietly, consistently, and reliably. But impatience led its owner to kill the goose in pursuit of immediate gain, destroying the very source of wealth. Property can function in the same way. A leveraged asset that produces income and appreciates steadily can build wealth over decades. Selling too early, simply because value has risen, can sacrifice a far greater long-term outcome.

A modern illustration of this can be seen in two investors facing similar choices. Emma sold her property after five years, locking in a £60,000 gain. After taxes and costs, she walked away satisfied. David, by contrast, refinanced his property instead of selling it. He released £40,000 of equity and reinvested it into another income-producing asset. A decade later, David still owned his original property and had doubled the size and value of his portfolio. Both decisions were profitable, but only one allowed leverage and time to compound together.

These examples highlight a critical truth: leverage is not just a tool for acquisition; it is a lifecycle strategy. It shapes how investors buy, hold, refinance, and exit. Every decision to sell, refinance, or retain an asset must be weighed not only against immediate gain, but against what is being given up: future income, future growth, and long-term optionality.

Leverage accelerates wealth creation, but it rests on something more fundamental. Before investors are willing to borrow against an asset, hold it through cycles, or pass it across generations, they must trust that the value they are building will endure.

This brings us to the next strength of property investing. Beyond income and leverage, property plays a deeper role in wealth creation: it acts as a reliable store of value. In the following chapter, we explore why property has preserved wealth across generations and why that matters just as much as how quickly it grows.

CHAPTER SUMMARY

The chapter illustrates how leverage allows investors to control larger assets, accelerate portfolio growth, and build wealth more quickly by using borrowed money responsibly and strategically.

KEY POINTS

- Leverage allows investors to control larger assets with less personal capital, accelerating portfolio growth beyond what cash alone can achieve.
- Good debt funds income producing or appreciating assets, while bad debt funds liabilities that do not generate returns.
- Leveraging multiple properties multiplies both rental income and capital appreciation compared to purchasing a single property outright.
- Negative equity becomes a risk when property values fall below outstanding mortgage balances, particularly during market downturns or when leverage is excessive.
- Refinancing enables investors to release equity, reduce borrowing costs, or restructure debt, provided cash flow remains resilient under different interest rate scenarios.
- Effective leverage requires monitoring loan to value ratios, stress testing affordability, and maintaining adequate financial reserves.
- Excessive leverage amplifies losses, restricts flexibility, and increases vulnerability to market shifts or interest rate changes.
- Leverage is a lifecycle strategy, supporting acquisition, growth, refinancing, and long-term wealth building when used with discipline and patience.

Enjoying this book?

I've created a free Property Investor Starter Pack exclusively for readers. It includes helpful tools and spreadsheets that you can use to analyse deals.

Download it free at: BuildWealthThroughProperty.com/start

Chapter 7 Property: A Store of Value

"Land is the one thing they're not making any more of." – Mark Twain

Over time, I began to notice a pattern. People who accumulated wealth through very different means—business owners, professionals, entrepreneurs, athletes, and even those who inherited money—often ended up doing the same thing with it. Regardless of how they made their wealth, many chose to store it in property. I wondered why.

For the truly wealthy, the challenge is not always about chasing higher returns or generating immediate income. More often, it is about preservation. The question shifts from how do I make more money? to how do I protect what I already have? In answering that question, property repeatedly emerged as the preferred solution. It became the place where value was parked, protected, and allowed to endure across time and economic cycles.

That realisation helped me understand one of property's most understated strengths: its ability, when approached correctly and held over the long term, to act as a reliable store of value.

WHAT DOES "STORE OF VALUE" REALLY MEAN?

A store of value is any asset that can retain and preserve its worth over time and be exchanged in the future without significant loss. Historically, gold, silver, and certain currencies have played this role. Property, however, particularly when purchased in areas with stable and consistent demand, has proven to be one of the most reliable stores of value available.

Unlike consumable or depreciating assets such as cars, electronics, or equipment, property does not disappear with use. The money invested in property is not spent or lost; it is captured within the asset itself. You can literally see where your money is! Whether you purchase outright or use a mortgage, the capital you committed to the purchase remains embedded in the bricks and mortar and can be realised later through refinancing or sale.

This distinction is subtle but powerful. Property doesn't merely generate returns, it holds wealth.

A PERSONAL REALISATION

I experienced this shift in understanding early in my own journey. At the time, I wasn't thinking in grand economic terms. I simply noticed that while markets fluctuated, interest rates changed, and personal circumstances evolved, property remained valuable.

The building aged, repairs were required, and tenants came and went, yet the value stored within the asset endured. The money that had gone into the property was not gone; it was sitting there quietly, protected within the bricks and mortar. It could not be stolen, it could not be moved, and it did not disappear with use.

Travelling around the United Kingdom makes this reality impossible to ignore. Buildings such as Hampton Court Palace, begun in 1515 and still standing over 500 years later, Shakespeare's Birthplace, built in 1564 and central to its town's identity, and

Stokesay Castle, which has endured for more than 700 years, remind us that property can outlast generations, wars, and economic systems. These structures continue to serve their communities through culture, employment, tourism, and shared heritage, demonstrating the enduring social and economic value of well-built property in the right locations.

This endurance underpins one of the core truths explored in book. When property is selected wisely and held with discipline, it is not merely a short-term investment but a long-term store of value—capable of preserving wealth, supporting communities, and transferring legacy across generations.

This perspective changed how I thought about money and property. Property was no longer just something that produced income month after month; it was a vessel that safeguarded capital across time. While currencies fluctuate and possessions wear out, well-built properties endure quietly, preserving value long after the original investment was made.

WHY PROPERTY STORES VALUE SO EFFECTIVELY

One of the fundamental reasons property stores value lies in scarcity. Land is finite. Unlike manufactured goods, it cannot be replicated or mass-produced. With the finite nature of land, large parts of the world are uninhabitable due to geography, climate, or environmental constraints. This means the land that is suitable for living, working, and commerce becomes increasingly valuable over time. As populations grow and urban areas expand, the availability of well-located land becomes increasingly constrained. This scarcity underpins long-term value.

Supply and demand further reinforce this effect. When demand for housing exceeds supply, a common reality in many cities, prices and rents are supported even during challenging economic periods. This imbalance helps property retain value when other assets struggle.

Property's tangible nature also matters. You can see it, use it, live in it, or rent it out. Unlike shares or digital assets, property has intrinsic utility. Even in uncertain times, people still need somewhere to live, work, and operate businesses. That utility gives property a resilience that purely financial instruments often lack.

Another key factor is the legal and regulatory framework surrounding property ownership. Established land registries[20], enforceable property rights, and well-defined legal systems provide confidence that ownership is protected. This institutional backing plays a significant role in property's ability to store value over long periods.

LIQUIDITY, STABILITY, AND DISCIPLINE

Property is not as liquid as stocks or bonds; it cannot be bought or sold instantly. Yet this relative illiquidity is often a strength rather than a weakness. It discourages panic selling and speculative trading, encouraging longer-term thinking and stability.

While property may take time to sell, properties located in well-located areas still hold their value stored and the equity be accessed without selling, through refinancing or equity release.

MANAGEMENT MATTERS

Of course, owning property alone is not enough. How it is managed plays a critical role in preserving value. Regular maintenance, appropriate insurance, and timely mortgage payments all contribute to protecting the asset.

Neglect can erode value surprisingly quickly. A poorly maintained property loses appeal, tenants, and ultimately worth. By contrast,

---

[20] Land registries: official public records that document legal ownership, boundaries, and interests in land and property.

even modest ongoing care helps preserve and sometimes enhance long-term value.

THE BIGGER PICTURE

Property's role as a store of value explains why it features so prominently in long-term wealth strategies. It preserves capital through economic cycles, holds purchasing power over time, and provides a foundation upon which other benefits income, leverage, and growth can be built.

This is why property is often where wealth ends up, even when it begins elsewhere.

CONCLUSION

Property is more than a means of generating income or accelerating growth. At its core, it is a vessel for preserving value. In a world where currencies fluctuate and many assets depreciate with use, property stands apart.

When well-chosen and properly managed, it quietly performs one of the most important roles in wealth building: it protects what you have already earned. And it is this ability to store value reliably over time that sets the stage for the next question every investor must ask.

Not just how wealth is preserved, but how it grows. In the next chapter, we move from preservation to progression, exploring why property is not only capable of holding value, but also of increasing it over time as an appreciating asset.

CHAPTER SUMMARY

This chapter explains that property is a powerful and reliable store of value because it preserves wealth over time through scarcity, tangible utility, stable demand, and enduring legal protection, often outlasting economic cycles and even generations.

KEY POINTS

- A store of value is an asset that retains and preserves its worth over time and can be exchanged in the future without significant loss. Property, particularly in areas with stable demand, is one of the most reliable stores of value.
- The finite nature of land and the continuous population growth contribute to the increasing value of property over time. As the world's population grows, the demand for habitable land increases, making property more valuable.
- When the demand for housing exceeds supply, property prices and rents are supported even during economic downturns. This imbalance helps property retain its value when other assets struggle.
- Unlike financial instruments, property has intrinsic utility. People always need places to live, work, and operate businesses, giving property a resilience that purely financial assets often lack.
- Established land registries, enforceable property rights, and well-defined legal systems provide confidence that ownership is protected, contributing to property's ability to store value over long periods.
- Property's relative illiquidity discourages panic selling and speculative trading, encouraging longer-term thinking and stability. Well-located properties hold their value, and equity can be accessed through refinancing or equity release.
- Proper management, including regular maintenance and appropriate insurance, is crucial for preserving property value. Neglect can quickly erode value, while ongoing care helps maintain and enhance long-term value.

Chapter 8 Property: An Appreciating Asset

"Long-term wealth is built by owning assets that grow while you sleep." — Anonymous

Property is widely regarded as an appreciating asset, something that not only holds its value but often increases in worth over time. This potential for long-term growth is one of the strongest reasons individuals, families, and institutions continue to invest in real estate. It is why it often becomes a cornerstone of wealth-building strategies and a foundational part of diversified portfolios. For me, this truth isn't just theoretical, it's personal.

My grandfather, who lived on another continent from me, was a committed real estate investor. He worked with the railway but invested in properties. He owned several substantial properties, at least five that I knew of, including large commercial buildings in a large city and multiple residential homes. These properties weren't just structures; they were long-term investments that continued to grow in value year after year.

Even after my grandfather passed away, his properties kept working. They continued to appreciate, they continued to generate income, and they continued to provide for the family he left behind. Because my father is no longer alive, my siblings and I still receive a small cheque every December, our share of the profit from my grandfather's real estate portfolio. It is a constant reminder that wealth built through property can outlive the person who created it.

My father, too, followed a similar path. Though not an investor in the same way, he understood the importance of owning property, and he ensured that the family homes would pass on to his children. In doing so, he preserved not only a physical asset but a sense of stability, continuity, and legacy.

This is the extraordinary nature of real estate: it grows, it endures, and it provides long after the original owner is gone. While property values may fluctuate in the short term influenced by the economy, interest rates, or changing market conditions, the long-term trend for well-chosen properties in desirable locations has historically been one of steady, reliable appreciation. When you invest in property, you are not just buying today's value; you are securing tomorrow's potential. One way that I like to explain this is that your property grows with you. As you age, so does the value of your property.

APPRECIATING VS. DEPRECIATING ASSETS

A depreciating asset is one whose value decreases over time, typically due to usage, wear and tear, and obsolescence. Examples include vehicles (though not really considered investment except classic vehicles) electronic devices, furniture, and machinery. These items lose value as they age or as newer and more efficient models enter the market.

In contrast, property, particularly land, and well-maintained buildings tend to retain or increase in value. Through regular maintenance, strategic improvements, and capital investment, property owners can extend the asset's life, enhance its desirability, and increase its market worth. This capacity for appreciation is what makes real estate one of the most effective long-term vehicles for wealth creation.

FORCES OF APPRECIATION: WHY PROPERTY VALUES RISE

Understanding why property values increase is essential for every property investor. Unlike shares traded on centralised exchanges, property operates within localised markets, each shaped by distinct economic, demographic, and social dynamics. Appreciation is therefore not random; it is the result of identifiable and often predictable forces.

At its core, property appreciation is driven by supply and demand. When demand for housing outpaces available supply, prices rise. This imbalance is commonly influenced by population growth, demographic shifts, employment opportunities, and the overall desirability of an area. Factors such as quality schools, access to amenities, safety, and lifestyle appeal all contribute to sustained demand.

Economic strength also plays a critical role. Areas characterised by stable employment, rising wages, and diverse local economies tend to experience stronger and more consistent property price growth. As household incomes increase, purchasing power expands, placing upward pressure on both property values and rental demand.

Infrastructure and development further accelerate appreciation. New transport links, educational institutions, healthcare facilities, and commercial hubs enhance accessibility and convenience, often transforming previously overlooked locations into sought-after areas. These improvements not only attract residents but also signal long-term government and private sector commitment to the area.

Government policy underpins many of these forces. Planning regulations, housing incentives, taxation, and interest-rate policy all influence supply, demand, and investor behaviour. Investors who remain informed about policy direction are better positioned to anticipate market shifts rather than simply react to them.

BUILDING WEALTH THROUGH EQUITY GROWTH

While appreciation increases a property's market value, the investor's true financial gain is reflected in equity. Equity[21] represents the portion of the property that the investor genuinely owns, calculated as the difference between the property's current market value and any outstanding mortgage balance.

This is where property investment becomes particularly powerful. Through the use of leverage, investors control 100% of the asset while contributing only a portion of the purchase price. As the property appreciates and the mortgage balance reduces over time, equity grows from two directions simultaneously.

Positive equity is a hallmark of a healthy investment. It provides financial stability, increases borrowing capacity, and creates opportunities for portfolio expansion. Conversely, negative equity where the mortgage exceeds the property's value, represents a risk that disciplined investors actively manage and avoid.

FORCING APPRECIATION: HOW INVESTORS ADD VALUE

Successful property investors do not rely solely on market forces; they actively create appreciation through strategic improvements and management. This process, often called forcing appreciation, involves making targeted changes that enhance a property's functionality, appeal, or income potential.

---

[21] Equity = Current Market Value − Outstanding Mortgage Balance
E.g. A property valued at £250,000 and mortgage balance is £50,000, the investor holds £200,000 in equity.

Common value-adding strategies include:

- Renovating key areas such as kitchens and bathrooms.
- Enhancing exterior appeal through landscaping and façade improvements.
- Reconfiguring interior layouts to maximise usable space.
- Adding practical amenities, such as parking or storage.
- Extending or converting areas to increase total floor space.

These improvements not only boost market value but can also increase rental income, improving the property's overall return on investment.

PROPERTY APPRECIATION IN THE UK: A LONG-TERM PERSPECTIVE

Property appreciation is best understood over decades, not years. In the UK, house prices have experienced cycles of growth, stagnation, and correction, yet the long-term trajectory has consistently been upward. Short-term volatility often dominates headlines simply because bad news sells, but long-term shows steady appreciation driven by population growth, constrained housing supply, inflation, and the enduring demand for shelter.

Over the past half century, UK residential property values have increased multiple times over in nominal terms, comfortably outpacing wage growth and, over long periods, preserving purchasing power against inflation. While there have been notable downturns—including the early 1990s recession and the 2008 financial crisis—each correction has been followed by recovery and new highs over time.

The key insight is not that property prices rise every year, but that well-located residential property has historically rewarded patience. Investors who purchased quality assets and held through market cycles benefited not from perfect timing, but from time itself. Appreciation, in this context, is not speculation but the cumulative outcome of long-term ownership in a structurally undersupplied market.

This is why property appreciation should be viewed as a function of duration and discipline, not market prediction. Property investment is unlike share investment, which is heavily influenced by speculation and market sentiment. Property value is grounded in real-world use, income, and long-term demand, making it structurally more stable over time. When combined with rental income, leverage applied prudently, and the ability to hold through downturns, capital growth becomes a powerful engine for wealth accumulation.

SIMPLE UK LONG-TERM TREND

Long-term UK house price data shows a clear upward trend over multiple decades, despite periodic corrections.

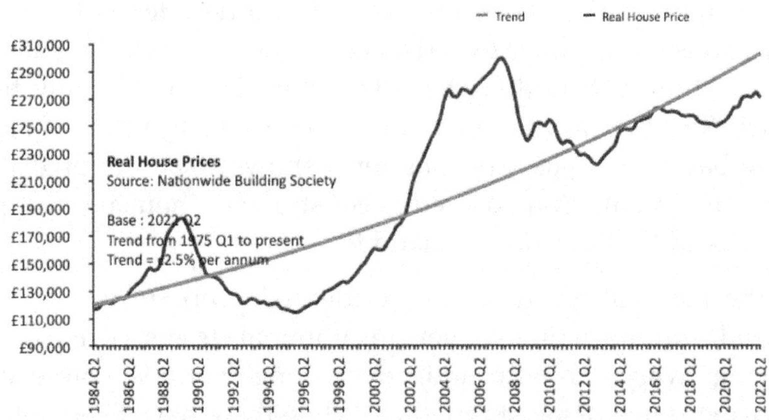

Figure 1:1: UK Real House Prices (1975–2022), showing long-term real growth trend of approximately 2.5% per annum. Source: Nationwide Building Society

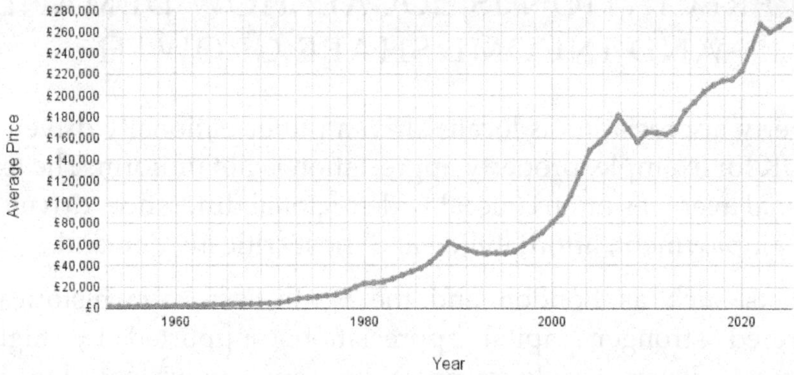

Figure 1:2: UK Average House Prices (1952–2022). Source: HM Land Registry, UK House Price Index.

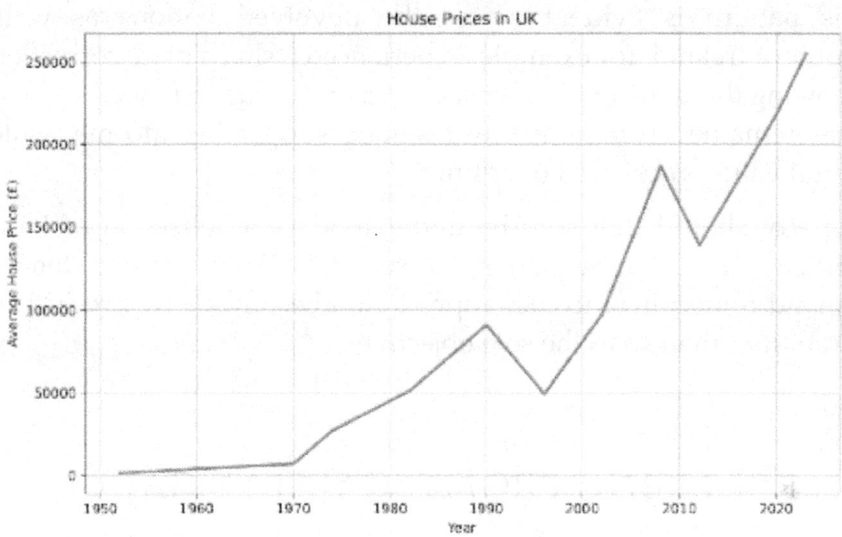

Figure 1:3: UK House Prices (1952–2023).

Data reflects nominal UK average house prices. Chart constructed by author using Nationwide quarterly series (1952–2023).

APPRECIATION IS LOCAL: HOW DEMAND AND INCOME SHAPE GROWTH

Property appreciation is locally driven rather nationally driven. In the UK for example, property appreciation is not uniform. The term national averages often conceal wide regional differences driven by local employment, affordability, and most critically demand.

Markets such as London and the South-East have historically delivered stronger capital appreciation, supported by higher incomes, dense employment hubs, and persistent housing shortages. Other regions have followed different paths, often offering much lower prices and stronger rental yields rather than rapid price growth.

This pattern is evident across the devolved nations as well. Northern Ireland, for example, experienced a sharp price correction following the 2008 financial crisis, yet rental demand in well-located areas remained comparatively resilient, supporting income while capital values recovered over time.

Property should therefore be understood as a collection of local markets, not a single national asset class. When strong tenant demand underpins income, appreciation becomes a by-product of durability rather than the sole objective.

REALISING PROFIT: CAPITAL GAINS

A capital gain occurs when a property is sold for more than its purchase price. The gain can arise naturally through long-term market growth or as a result of value-adding improvements. However, it is important to distinguish between realised and unrealised gains.

Unrealised (Paper) Gain

The increase in property value while it remains unsold. It enhances your net worth and can be leveraged for further borrowing or reinvestment, but it is not cash in hand.

Realised Gain

The profit you make once the property is sold representing actual financial return after deducting all costs, including purchase, improvements, and taxes.

The ultimate objective for any property investor is to manage assets in a way that maximises total return combining rental income, equity growth, and capital appreciation while strategically timing sales to achieve the greatest possible capital gain.

As you've seen, one of the most remarkable qualities of property is its ability to grow in value over time. Appreciation turns a single purchase into a long-term wealth-building engine, often working quietly in the background as life carries on. But appreciation does more than simply increase your net worth — it also protects it.

Because while property values rise over the years, something else is rising too: the cost of living. Inflation slowly eats away at the purchasing power of money, reducing what it can buy and eroding savings if they're left standing still. Yet property behaves differently. Instead of being weakened by inflation, it often strengthens because of it.

So, as we move into the next chapter, we shift from property's ability to grow your wealth to its ability to protect your wealth. Let's explore how real estate acts as a powerful shield giving you an edge against inflation and helping your money keep its value in a world where prices are always changing.

CHAPTER SUMMARY

This chapter shows that property is a uniquely powerful wealth builder because it consistently appreciates over time—driven by demand, scarcity, local economic forces, and value adding opportunities—allowing investors to grow equity and long term wealth across generations.

KEY POINTS

- Property is an appreciating asset, meaning its value tends to rise over time, especially in strong locations.
- Long term appreciation is driven by population growth, demand outpacing supply, economic strength, and infrastructure development.
- Appreciation is different from depreciation: buildings can wear out, but well maintained property and land generally increase in value.
- Appreciation happens due to local factors, not national averages—property markets are local, not uniform.
- Investors grow wealth through equity, which increases both as mortgages are repaid and as property prices rise.
- Investors can also force appreciation by adding value through renovations, reconfiguration, extensions, and upgrades.
- UK long term data shows values rise despite short term fluctuations, proving the importance of holding property through economic cycles.
- Capital gains are realised upon sale, but appreciation also builds unrealised wealth that can be leveraged for further investments.

Chapter 9
Property: A Hedge Against Inflation

"Inflation is taxation without legislation." — Milton Friedman

Inflation is one of those things we feel long before we fully understand it. We notice it when our weekly shopping costs more than it used to, or when our energy bills rise even though our usage hasn't changed.

The UK's recent cost-of-living crisis made this painfully clear. Prices surged across the board — food, energy, transport, rent, and everyday essentials — reaching a 41-year high of 11.1% in 2022, driven largely by the after-effects of the pandemic and the war in Ukraine. Many families simply could not keep up.

With the cost-of-living crisis being a trending topic at the time, it was discussed in my daughter's school, and she explained inflation in the simplest and most memorable way. She said:

"Inflation is when the money that used to buy bread before isn't enough to buy the same bread today."

A perfect illustration of a complex economic reality.

Inflation is, at its core, the erosion of purchasing power. It means that the same amount of money buys less as time goes on. When prices rise faster than wages, families feel the strain, savings lose real value, and financial security becomes fragile. This has been the lived experience of millions, where rising costs have consistently outpaced income growth.

Inflation is also defined more formally as the sustained increase in the general price level of goods and services within an economy, typically measured on an annual basis. Over time, inflation reduces the purchasing power of money, making it a critical concept for investors to understand.

Economists distinguish between two key measures of value. Nominal value refers to the face value of money, while real value reflects its true purchasing power once inflation is considered. Understanding the difference between nominal and real value is essential when assessing investment performance, particularly in periods of rising prices.

£100 this year may still be £100 four years later, but its real value has fallen if prices have risen. In the UK, the Office for National Statistics (ONS) tracks these changes using a representative "basket" of goods and services to calculate the inflation rate.

Understanding this impact is vital because it highlights one of the greatest financial threats people face and one of the strongest reasons properties remains such a powerful asset. I once asked a group of men at a retreat:

"What are you doing to ensure that the money you're saving for retirement will still support your lifestyle in the future, knowing full well that inflation will weaken it?"

It's a question every one of us must confront. Because while inflation quietly eats away at the value of cash, property often behaves very differently and that makes all the difference.

Unlike cash, which weakens as prices rise, property often moves in the opposite direction. As the cost-of-living increases, rents and property values typically rise as well, providing a natural defence against inflation. In a world where money steadily loses power, property stands strong — one of the most reliable shields against the forces that erode wealth.

In the context of investing, property has long been recognised as an effective hedge against inflation. But to appreciate why, it helps to first understand the nature of inflation itself and how it affects everyday life.

CAUSES OF INFLATION

Inflation typically arises from two key sources: cost-push inflation and demand-pull inflation.

Cost-Push Inflation:

Occurs when the cost of production for goods and services rise for example, due to higher prices for raw materials, labour, or energy. Businesses often pass these costs on to consumers, leading to an overall increase in prices.

Demand-Pull Inflation:

Happens when overall demand in the economy increases faster than supply. When demand exceeds available goods and services, prices are driven upward. To manage inflation, most economies rely on their central banks, such as the Bank of England, which adjusts interest rates to influence borrowing and spending. Higher interest rates make borrowing more expensive and saving more attractive, reducing consumer demand and, in turn, slowing the rate of inflation.

THE LONG-TERM APPRECIATION TREND

One of the key reasons property is considered an effective inflation hedge lies in its historical trend of long-term appreciation. Over many decades, real estate has consistently increased in value, often outpacing inflation.

In the UK, property prices have risen significantly over the past two decades. While short-term fluctuations occur due to market cycles, long-term data shows that residential property values have consistently trended upward. Over extended periods, real estate has generally appreciated at a rate that outpaces inflation, reinforcing its role as a long-term store of value.

This long-term appreciation ensures that property investors not only preserve their capital in real terms but often experience real growth in wealth even during periods of rising inflation.

INTRINSIC VALUE: THE FOUNDATION OF PROPERTY'S STABILITY

Unlike purely financial instruments such as bonds, treasury bills, certificates of deposit, derivatives, or exchange-traded funds (ETFs), property is a tangible asset with inherent, or intrinsic, value.

Financial assets typically derive their worth from contractual obligations and market sentiment rather than physical characteristics. Their value can fluctuate significantly with changes in interest rates and inflation. For example, when inflation rises, the real return on fixed-interest investments (like bonds or savings accounts) often declines because their nominal returns do not increase in line with inflation.

Property, however, derives its value from physical and practical factors such as location, size, construction quality, and usefulness. These tangible qualities provide inherent worth that is far less sensitive to inflationary pressures or short-term market swings. Even when broader markets fluctuate, well-maintained and strategically located properties tend to hold or increase in value.

In other words, the intrinsic value of property acts as a stabilising anchor. While financial assets may lose real value during inflationary periods, real estate continues to offer both utility (as housing or commercial space) and long-term capital appreciation.

INFLATION-PROTECTED INCOME STREAMS

Certain property investments are structured to adjust in line with inflation, helping investors preserve the real value of their income over time. This is typically achieved through contractual or structural mechanisms that link rental growth to inflationary measures.

COMMERCIAL LEASES

Many commercial lease agreements include rent review clauses that are indexed to the Consumer Price Index (CPI[22]). These provisions allow rental income to increase in step with inflation, providing a degree of protection against the erosion of purchasing power.

REAL ESTATE INVESTMENT TRUSTS (REITS)

REITs typically hold diversified portfolios of income-producing properties. As rents across these portfolios adjust over time, distributions can also increase, helping investors benefit from inflation-linked income growth. This structure can offer both income resilience and capital preservation during inflationary periods.

---

[22] The Consumer Price Index (CPI) is a measure of inflation that tracks changes over time in the prices of a representative basket of goods and services consumed by households and is widely used as an indicator of changes in the cost of living.

LOCATION: THE DECIDING FACTOR

While property generally acts as a hedge against inflation, location remains the single most important determinant of performance. This truth was famously captured by Harold Samuel, founder of Land Securities, who, when asked what mattered most in property, replied: "Location, location, location." His answer endures because of the permanence of location. Buildings can be refurbished, finance can be restructured, and strategies can evolve but location is fixed.

Properties situated in high-demand areas particularly those with strong transport links, quality schools, and access to employment are far more likely to retain and grow in value during inflationary periods. Demand in such locations remains resilient even as costs rise, allowing rents and capital values to adjust upward over time.

Conversely, properties in declining or low-demand areas may struggle to keep pace with inflation or, in real terms, lose value altogether. Strategic investors therefore prioritise prime locations and emerging growth regions when building their portfolios, ensuring that inflation works for them, not against them.

SUMMARY

Property serves as a powerful inflation hedge because it combines tangible intrinsic value, income growth potential, and historical long-term appreciation.

While inflation erodes the purchasing power of cash and diminishes the real return on fixed-income assets such as bonds, funds and shares, well-chosen property investments tend to rise in value and generate increasing rental income. This dual benefit protection and growth is what makes property one of the most resilient and enduring assets in any inflationary environment.

When you combine income, leverage, appreciation, and protection against inflation, property becomes one of the most robust wealth-building tools available. But the true power of real estate becomes even clearer when you discover how the system works with you, not against you.

Governments encourage investment in housing, and as a result, property investors enjoy a range of tax advantages that can significantly boost long-term returns.

Next, we explore these benefits and how they allow property to build wealth not just through what you earn, but through what you legally keep.

CHAPTER SUMMARY

This chapter explains that property acts as a powerful hedge against inflation because both rents and property values tend to rise with the cost of living, preserving and often increasing an investor's real purchasing power over time.

KEY POINTS

- Inflation erodes the purchasing power of money, making cash worth less over time.
- Property typically **rises in value during inflationary periods**, often outpacing general price increases.
- Rental income also tends to increase with inflation, providing an **inflation protected cash flow**.
- Property has **intrinsic value**—people always need places to live and work—making it more resilient than purely financial assets.
- Because land is scarce and demand for housing is persistent, property prices are naturally supported during inflation.
- Commercial leases often include **inflation linked rent reviews**, protecting income in line with CPI or market conditions.
- Location remains critical: properties in high demand areas retain value and benefit most from inflation-driven growth.
- Property protects wealth while other assets (like savings or fixed income instruments) lose value when inflation rises.
- Rising construction costs during inflation also push up replacement costs, indirectly supporting existing property values.

Chapter 10
Property: Tax Benefits

"In this world nothing can be said to be certain, except death and taxes." — Benjamin Franklin

This chapter does not seek to provide tax advice or capture every rate or allowance in force at a given moment in time. Instead, it focuses on structural principles and decision frameworks that have remained consistent despite frequent changes in tax policy. Readers should always confirm current rates and rules with professional advisers before acting.

Every form of commercial activity operates within a defined legal and fiscal environment. In some jurisdictions, such as U.A.E, rental income from property is not subject to personal income tax, although transaction charges apply at purchase. In others, such as Monaco or the Cayman Islands, income tax may be absent while costs arise through fees, duties, or ownership structures. By contrast, countries like the United Kingdom and the United States tax property income directly but allow deductions, reliefs, and structuring opportunities.

The form taxation takes differs by jurisdiction, but property investment does not exist outside government systems. Charges may arise at acquisition, during ownership, or on transfer. Property generates income, creates value, and involves regulation, meaning investors must be informed about where and how costs and obligations apply within each market.

The real distinction, however, lies not in whether tax is paid, but in how much control the individual has over it. There was a time when a good portion of my income came from an earned salary. Like many people, I worked hard, progressed professionally, and earned more over time. Yet no matter how much I earned, tax was deducted before the money ever reached me and I like to joke that the government doesn't trust employees, so they tax employment at source. There was very little room to plan, structure, or defer. My income increased, but so did my tax bill.

PROPERTY – A DIFFERENT DYNAMIC

Property introduced a different dynamic. Unlike earned income, property allows investors to plan. With the right structure, legitimate costs can be offset, income can be timed, and profits can be reinvested rather than immediately extracted and taxed. Proper tax planning does not remove tax, nor is it about evasion. It is about paying tax efficiently and intentionally, in a way that supports long-term wealth creation rather than working against it.

Governments use tax systems to influence behaviour. Housing supply, regeneration, and long-term investment are economic priorities for the government, and property investors play a vital role in delivering them. As a result, property is supported by a framework of tax rules that, when understood, can work in the investor's favour.

To benefit from this advantage, investors must first understand the tax landscape they are operating within. Property is subject to several taxes at different stages of the investment journey—when buying, while holding, and when selling—and each of these affects returns in different ways.

The next section breaks down the key taxes every property investor must understand, providing the foundation for effective planning and informed decision-making. Property is not tax-free, but it offers far more control over taxation than earned income ever will.

THE TAXES EVERY PROPERTY INVESTOR MUST UNDERSTAND

Every property investment operates within a tax environment. From the moment you buy, through the years you hold, and eventually when you sell or pass assets on, taxation quietly shapes your results. Understanding these taxes is not about avoiding obligations; it is about making informed decisions that allow you to retain more of what you earn and compound wealth over time. In property, tax efficiency is rarely accidental. It is the result of foresight, structure, and alignment between strategy and legislation. Broadly speaking, property taxes fall into three stages of the investment journey: entry, ownership, and exit. Let's explore further.

Taxes at the Point of Purchase

When acquiring property, one of the most immediate tax considerations is stamp duty, also referred to in some regions as transfer tax, property acquisition tax, or registration duty. This is a cost payable upfront and therefore directly affects your entry price and overall returns. For investors in the U.K, it is particularly significant because additional properties often attract higher rates. Buy-to-let purchases and properties acquired through limited companies are commonly subject to surcharges. My view is simple: treat it as the cost of securing your place in the property market — the price of having a piece of the property pie.

Taxes During Ownership

Once a property is owned, taxation becomes an ongoing consideration, though the form it takes varies by jurisdiction and ownership structure. In some regions, rental income may not be subject to personal income tax, while in others it is treated in the same way as earned income.

In the UK context, where property is held personally, rental income is taxed as personal income. Allowable running costs can reduce taxable profit, but mortgage interest is no longer fully deductible.

Instead, landlords receive a flat-rate tax credit, a change that has altered the economics of personal ownership, particularly for higher-rate taxpayers.

Also, within the UK, when property is owned through a limited company, rental income is treated as business income. Mortgage interest and running costs are fully deductible before tax, and profits are subject to Corporation Tax rather than personal income tax. This structural difference is one of the key reasons many UK portfolio investors favour corporate ownership, especially where profits are reinvested rather than extracted.

Taxes at the Point of Exit

When a property is sold, any increase in value may be subject to capital gains taxation, depending on the jurisdiction and ownership structure. In some regions, such gains are not taxed, while in others they can materially reduce the net proceeds of a sale.

In the UK context, individuals are subject to Capital Gains Tax, which can significantly reduce net returns, particularly for higher-rate taxpayers. Where property is held through a company, gains are taxed within the corporate structure, often allowing greater flexibility around timing, offsetting costs, and reinvestment.

Exit taxes are frequently overlooked at the point of purchase, yet they can have one of the largest impacts on lifetime investment returns. Smart investors consider their exit strategy early and plan accordingly, rather than treating taxation as an afterthought.

KEY TAX ADVANTAGES

In jurisdictions where property is subject to taxation, it can at first appear heavily taxed. There may be charges to consider at acquisition, during ownership, and on disposal. For many people, this is where the conversation about property tax ends. But this is only half the picture.

What makes property different is not the absence of tax, but the flexibility within the system. Unlike many other forms of income, property often allows investors to manage their tax position legitimately through structure, allowances, and long-term planning.

This is where property comes into its own. In this section, we'll explore the key tax advantages available to property investors and why, using the UK as a practical example, property remains one of the most tax-efficient ways to build wealth when approached correctly.

Mortgage Interest Deductions

One of the most significant tax considerations for property investors is the treatment of mortgage interest. In many countries, interest paid on borrowing for an investment property is treated as a legitimate business expense and may be deducted from taxable rental income, reducing the overall tax liability.

In the UK, however, this position has changed. Prior to 2017, individual landlords were able to deduct 100 per cent of mortgage interest from their rental income. Following the phased introduction of Section 24, mortgage interest can no longer be deducted in full. Instead, landlords receive a basic-rate tax credit of 20 per cent, regardless of whether they are basic-rate or higher-rate taxpayers.

Limited companies are not subject to this restriction. Unlike individual landlords, companies are generally able to deduct the full cost of mortgage interest as a business expense before tax is calculated. This distinction can materially improve cash flow and has made the company structure a more viable option for leveraged property investment.

The impact of these different treatments is best understood in practice. The following example compares the outcomes across ownership structures of basic-rate taxpayer, a higher taxpayer and a SPV[23].

Worked Example: Comparing Tax Outcomes Across Ownership Structures

Common assumptions (same property in all cases)

Annual rental income: £20,000

Mortgage interest (interest-only): £8,000

Other allowable costs: £2,000

Basic-rate income tax: 20%

Higher-rate income tax: 40%

Corporation Tax (SPV): 25%

Section 24 fully in effect

Option 1: Personal Ownership – Basic-Rate Taxpayer

Item	Amount (£)
Rental income	20,000
Less: allowable costs (excluding interest)	(2,000)
Taxable profit	**18,000**
Income tax at 20%	(3,600)
Section 24 tax credit (20% of £8,000)	+1,600
Net tax payable	2,000
Less: mortgage interest	(8,000)
Net cash position	**£8,000**

[23] A Special Purpose Vehicle (SPV) is a limited company established solely to acquire and manage property assets, allowing investors to ring-fence risk and simplify lending and tax treatment (HM Revenue & Customs, 2023). It can be used to hold either a single property or a defined property portfolio. It separates ownership, liabilities, and cash flows from other assets, enabling risk isolation, clearer accounting, and structured joint ventures. Whether used per property or across a portfolio, an SPV allows investors to assess performance accurately and scale with discipline and transparency.

Option 2: Personal Ownership – Higher-Rate Taxpayer

Item	Amount (£)
Rental income	20,000
Less: allowable costs (excluding interest)	(2,000)
Taxable profit	**18,000**
Income tax at 40%	(7,200)
Section 24 tax credit (20% of £8,000)	+1,600
Net tax payable	5,600
Less: mortgage interest	(8,000)
Net cash position	**£4,400**

Option 3: Limited Company (SPV)

Item	Amount (£)
Rental income	20,000
Less: mortgage interest	(8,000)
Less: other allowable costs	(2,000)
Taxable profit	10,000
Corporation Tax at 25%	(2,500)
Net profit retained in company	£7,500

(Personal tax may arise later if profits are extracted as salary or dividends.)

What this comparison shows clearly is that basic-rate taxpayers are broadly neutral under Section 24 but still lose full interest deductibility. Higher-rate taxpayers experience the greatest cash-flow erosion under personal ownership. SPV ownership restores interest deductibility, producing more stable post-tax results for leveraged portfolios, particularly where profits are reinvested rather than immediately extracted. This is why many portfolio investors now buy through a limited company SPVs.

Allowable Expenses and Deductions

Property investors can reduce their taxable income by deducting the legitimate costs involved in running and maintaining a rental property. Expenses such as management or letting agent fees, routine maintenance and repairs, insurance, service charges, and professional fees all reduce the amount of profit subject to tax. In some cases, costs associated with marketing a property or travelling for inspections and management purposes may also be allowable.

By claiming these deductions correctly, investors ensure they are taxed only on their true profit, rather than on gross rental income. This distinction is crucial. It allows property to be treated as a real investment, where costs are recognised, and tax is applied fairly to what remains.

For example, consider a rental property that generates £15,000 in annual rent. If the landlord incurs £4,000 in allowable running costs, such as management fees, maintenance, insurance, and professional services, only the remaining £11,000 is subject to tax. The investor is therefore taxed on the true profit of the property, not on the total rent received.

This is one of the key reasons property investing can be so tax efficient. Legitimate costs are recognised, and tax is applied only after the property has paid for running and keeping itself.

Capital Gains Tax Reliefs

Another important consideration for property investors is how capital gains are treated. When a property is sold for more than its purchase price, the resulting profit—known as a capital gain—is generally subject to Capital Gains Tax (CGT). However, with careful planning, the amount of tax payable can often be reduced.

In the UK, individuals benefit from an annual CGT exemption, allowing a portion of capital gains to be realised each tax year without incurring CGT. Any gain above this allowance is taxed at rates that depend on the investor's income level and the nature of the asset. The timing of a disposal can therefore play an important role in managing overall tax exposure.

Further relief may be available where a property has previously been used as a main residence. In such cases, Private Residence Relief can reduce or eliminate CGT on the portion of the gain attributable to periods of occupation.

Capital Gains Tax rules have also evolved in recent years, with changes to rates and allowances in 2024 and 2025 highlighting the UK government's readiness to adjust property taxation in response to wider fiscal pressures. While specific rates are beyond the scope of this book, these developments reinforce a broader principle: tax policy is inherently fluid, and investment decisions are best structured to remain robust under changing tax regimes.

Depreciation and Capital Allowances

While land generally does not depreciate, the buildings and fixtures on it do. Tax systems in several countries allow investors to deduct depreciation or capital allowances, as it is referred to, on the cost of the structure, furnishings, and certain improvements.

This non-cash expense allows investors to reduce their taxable income without reducing their actual cash flow. For example, in the UK, landlords may claim capital allowances on items such as heating systems, alarms, and furniture in furnished rentals. In the US and Canada, depreciation deductions can be substantial, allowing investors to write down property values over decades. Depreciation is a powerful tool: it defers taxes, increases short-term cash flow, and enhances after-tax returns.

Tax Benefits for Limited Companies and Incorporation

Many property investors choose to hold their properties through a limited company rather than in their personal name. This structure can offer meaningful tax and strategic advantages, particularly as a portfolio grows. In the UK, profits earned within a company are subject to Corporation Tax, which is charged at a flat rate and is often lower than the higher and additional personal income tax rates. This can result in a lower overall tax burden for investors whose rental income would otherwise push them into higher tax brackets.

As previously noted, the company structure also differs from personal ownership in how financing costs are treated, which can materially affect cash flow and investment viability. Beyond taxation, holding property within a company allows profits to be retained and reinvested efficiently. Rather than drawing income personally and triggering additional income tax, investors can leave profits inside the company and use them as deposits or working capital for future acquisitions, enabling faster and more controlled portfolio growth.

Company ownership can also simplify estate planning and succession. Properties may be transferred through changes in shareholding rather than direct property sales, offering greater flexibility and control over how assets are passed to future generations. While incorporation involves setup costs, ongoing compliance, and administrative responsibilities, for investors building larger or long-term portfolios, a limited company structure can be both strategically advantageous and structurally efficient over time.

Inheritance Tax (IHT) and Wealth Transfer

Property is a long-term wealth vehicle, and effective planning can minimise inheritance tax (IHT) burdens on future generations. Through trusts, company structures, or gifting strategies, investors can pass assets efficiently to heirs while minimising estate tax liabilities. Some investors also use life insurance policies or business relief mechanisms to ensure their estates remain solvent and protected. Professional advice is crucial here, as inheritance laws and exemptions vary between countries—and poor planning can result in significant tax exposure.

Tax Relief for Energy Efficiency and Renovation

Many governments now offer tax incentives to encourage sustainable development and energy-efficient property improvements. Investors who upgrade their properties to meet modern energy standards can often access valuable financial benefits. These may include tax deductions for improvements such as insulation upgrades, renewable energy installations, or more efficient heating systems. In some cases, energy-efficient buildings may also qualify for reduced council tax or business rates, helping to lower ongoing ownership costs.

In addition, grants or special allowances are sometimes available to support the retrofitting of older properties, making it more affordable to improve performance and compliance. Beyond the immediate tax advantages, these improvements often enhance a property's long-term value, reduce running costs, and increase its appeal to environmentally conscious tenants. In this way, sustainability becomes not just a social responsibility, but a strategic and financially rewarding investment decision.

THE IMPORTANCE OF PROFESSIONAL TAX PLANNING

Tax regulations are complex and frequently changing. What is advantageous today may shift with government policy tomorrow. Therefore, successful property investors work closely with qualified accountants, tax advisers, or financial planners to structure ownership effectively, maximise deductions and reliefs, stay compliant with all reporting requirements and legally minimise overall tax liability.

Proper tax planning is not about avoidance, it is about optimisation, ensuring that every decision supports long-term financial growth.

SUMMARY

Tax benefits are one of the most powerful tools available to property investors. From mortgage interest relief and depreciation deductions to capital gains exemptions and company structures, the tax system provides numerous ways to enhance returns and preserve wealth.

When combined with capital appreciation, rental income, and the intrinsic value of real estate, these tax advantages make property investment one of the most strategically rewarding and resilient wealth-building vehicles available.

As we conclude on all things tax, no investor succeeds alone. Behind every tax-efficient portfolio stands a skilled accountant, a smart broker, a diligent solicitor, and a well-structured team. Tax efficiency may save you money, but the right team will make you money. In the next chapter, we explore how to build your Property Power Team, the experts who protect your wealth, accelerate your growth, and ensure every investment moves you toward financial freedom.

CHAPTER SUMMARY

This chapter shows that tax benefits make property one of the most strategically powerful wealth building tools by allowing investors to reduce taxable income, structure ownership efficiently, and legally retain more of what their investments earn over time.

KEY POINTS

- Property is taxed at three stages—when buying, during ownership, and when selling—and understanding these taxes helps investors plan efficiently.
- Unlike employment income, where tax is deducted at source, property income offers flexibility, allowing costs to be offset and income to be structured strategically.
- During ownership, rental income may be taxable, but allowable expenses (maintenance, management, insurance, etc.) can reduce the taxable amount.
- Section 24 in the UK restricts mortgage interest relief for individuals, but limited companies can deduct full mortgage interest, improving cash flow.
- Investors can benefit from capital allowances or depreciation, which reduce taxable profit without reducing actual cash flow.
- Company structures (SPVs) can offer lower tax rates, full interest deductibility, reinvestment benefits, and smoother succession planning.
- Inheritance tax planning, through trusts, shares, or structured ownership, helps protect wealth for future generations.
- Governments often incentivise property investment through energy efficiency tax credits, grants, and reliefs for upgrades.
- Effective property taxation relies on professional advice and proper structuring to ensure compliance while maximising long term returns.

Chapter 11
Building Your Property Investment Team

"If you want to go fast, go alone. If you want to go far, go together."
– African Proverb

Property investment is not a solo pursuit. Behind every successful investor is a reliable team of professionals whose expertise help avoid costly mistakes and maximise returns. Each member of your team plays a unique and important role, and together they form the foundation of your success.

The reality is that it can take time to assemble your "power team". While you may find capable service providers online, I've found that asking people in my network for referrals, especially from those who have had positive experiences, is often more effective. In addition, responding promptly, whether by providing requested information or making timely payments, helps build strong relationships. These habits encourage trust, foster goodwill, and ultimately lead to better service.

THE MORTGAGE BROKER

A good independent mortgage broker is invaluable. They

understand lending criteria, interest rates, and the fine print of finance deals that most investors overlook. A broker's job is to help you secure the best mortgage product for your circumstances - one that balances affordability, flexibility, and long-term growth. A skilled broker can also advise when to fix or track your rate, how to structure loans for multiple properties, and how to maintain your borrowing power as your portfolio grows.

When I bought my first house, I simply walked into my local bank. Their in-house mortgage advisor offered me a rate, I accepted it, and then I went off to find a property. At the time, I didn't know there was any other way of doing it.

It wasn't until I started dealing with estate agents that I discovered many of them also work with mortgage brokers, often called independent mortgage advisers. When I came to buy my second home, I decided to use the adviser recommended by the estate agent. This wasn't by accident; it was a strategic move. I wanted to be seen as a serious and preferred buyer for the property I was after.

The real lesson here is this: your local bank can only sell you its own products, and those products may not be the best fit. Some banks, for example, limit the number of buy-to-let mortgages you can hold with them. If you're planning to build a property portfolio, it makes sense to think ahead and choose a lender you can grow with—often a specialist buy-to-let bank rather than a traditional high-street one.

THE ESTATE AGENT

Estate agents, estate agents, estate agents. They are a critical part of the property ecosystem. At their best, they are the eyes and ears of the market and can be an invaluable resource for investors. At their worst, however, some lack depth in local knowledge, fail to understand investor criteria, or operate purely transactionally rather than strategically. Every investor dreams of having an agent who calls them first when a great deal comes along — before it ever reaches the open market.

That said, real estate is a regulated market, and agents must ensure that everyone has a fair opportunity to view and purchase. However, there are occasions such as when a seller is distressed and time is of the essence, where a quick, decisive sale is the priority. This is where strong relationships matter, along with your ability to act promptly and have your "gunpowder" ready.

In addition, the best agents understand both the numbers and the neighbourhoods in which they operate. They know what tenants are looking for and the premium that buyers are willing to pay. This kind of insight is invaluable to you as an investor.

Build genuine relationships with agents. When they know you are serious, reliable, and ready to act, they will treat you accordingly.

THE SOLICITOR OR CONVEYANCER

Every property transaction comes with legal details that must be handled correctly. This is where a property solicitor (or conveyancer) becomes essential. They ensure contracts, searches, and compliance requirements are all in order, protect your interests, manage the transfer of ownership, and help you understand exactly what you're signing.

I've found that working with solicitors who are property investors themselves can be a real advantage. Their first-hand experience and genuine interest in property often help uncover potential issues early, avoid hidden liabilities, and reduce unnecessary delays.

THE ACCOUNTANT

A good accountant can become one of your strongest long-term allies. I've learned that property investment brings with it a whole layer of tax complexity from stamp duty and allowable expenses to capital gains and inheritance planning (see above). Not all accountants are the same. While any accountant can help with basic accounting needs, those with real experience in property make a noticeable difference. An accountant who understands real estate can help structure your portfolio in a tax-efficient and fully compliant way, ensuring you keep more of what you earn. They can also guide you on whether it makes sense to hold properties in your own name or through a limited company, depending on your long-term strategy.

THE PROPERTY MANAGER

If you don't plan to manage your properties personally, appoint a reliable property manager or letting agent. A good manager handles tenant screening, rent collection, maintenance, and legal compliance. They can also keep you updated on market trends and rent reviews. While they charge a fee (typically 8–15% of rent), they free up your time to focus on strategy rather than day-to-day issues. Note that some of them will charge you additional fees when they have to arrange for a handyman or maintenance person to attend to your property.

THE SURVEYOR

A professional surveyor assesses a property's condition and value. Their report helps you identify potential repair costs before you buy and can also support your financing application. An independent opinion from a surveyor ensures you don't overpay and protects you from costly surprises after purchase.

If you're buying a property with a mortgage, the lender will require a survey. You usually have the choice of relying on the lender's basic valuation or commissioning a more detailed survey yourself, depending on the level of reassurance you want, your experience with property, and the type and state of property you're buying. A detailed survey is often necessary; you can also use this to renegotiate the price, even after you have agreed on it.

THE BUILDER

A builder is responsible for capital works, projects that materially change, improve, or extend the property. This includes refurbishments, conversions, extensions, structural alterations, and compliance upgrades. Builders are central to value-add strategies, where equity is created through improvement rather than market movement alone.

A competent builder does more than construct. They translate drawings into reality, manage tradespeople, sequence works correctly, and understand building control requirements. Their work directly affects timelines, budgets, valuations, and mortgage drawdowns.

Choosing a builder on price alone is a costly mistake, one I learned the hard way. A good builder must be reliable, efficient, experienced, and conversant with building regulations. Reliability, proven experience on similar projects, financial stability, and clear communication matter far more than the cheapest quote. A delayed project or a poorly executed build can erase years of projected returns. The truth is that there are many builders out there who have no idea of what they are doing. Entire television programs exist solely to document the damage caused by poor builders. These are not rare, isolated incidents but recurring patterns that underline the cost of choosing wrongly[24]. A good builder is worth their weight in gold.

THE HANDYMAN

A handyman plays a different but equally vital role. They handle minor repairs, maintenance, and react to issues that arise during

[24] UK consumer affairs television programmes such as *Cowboy Builders* and *Rogue Traders* document repeated cases of poor workmanship, abandoned building projects, and significant financial loss caused by unvetted or dishonest contractors.

occupation. Dripping taps, broken fixtures, damaged doors, small electrical or plumbing issues, these do not require a builder, but they do require prompt attention.

The handyman protects cash flow by keeping properties functional, tenants satisfied, and small problems from becoming expensive ones. Speed and availability matter more here than scale. A good handyman is dependable, cost-effective, and familiar with your properties.

Note that a builder is not a handyman and blurring these roles creates inefficiency and unnecessary cost. Using a builder for minor repairs is expensive. Using a handyman for structural work is risky and often non-compliant.

THE MENTOR OR EXPERIENCED INVESTOR

While not always an official member of your team, having a mentor or trusted advisor can accelerate your growth. A seasoned property investor can share lessons, contacts, and insights that only experience can teach. Surrounding yourself with people who have already achieved what you're aiming for helps you make better, more confident decisions. And of course, continue to invest in education just as you have in purchasing this book.

BRINGING IT ALL TOGETHER

The key to building a strong property team is communication and alignment. Everyone you work with should understand your goals, timelines, and appetite for risk. Treat your team members as long-term partners, not just service providers. Keep in touch regularly, update them on your progress, and listen to their advice—it's what you're paying for.

When your team shares your vision, your investments become smoother, faster, and more profitable. Property investing is far less stressful when you are not doing everything alone.

FINAL THOUGHT

A great team doesn't just support your success; it multiplies it. When every professional on your side understands your goals and delivers quality advice, you'll find that your investments grow more predictably and profitably. One mistake that I have made and see others make is looking for cheap services. Whilst I don't want to overpay for any service, I have since understood that you get what you pay for. I have paid for cheap services, only to have to pay again, because the job wasn't properly done. I now try to pay for quality once.

In property, relationships are as valuable as the bricks themselves. Build wisely, stay consistent, and surround yourself with excellence because the right people will help turn your "why" into lasting wealth.

CHAPTER SUMMARY

This chapter shows that property investment is a team driven journey, where success depends on surrounding yourself with the right professionals—brokers, agents, solicitors, accountants, managers, and mentors—who help you avoid costly mistakes, strengthen decisions, and accelerate long term growth.

KEY POINTS

- Property investing is not a solo venture; every successful investor relies on a strong and reliable team.
- A skilled mortgage broker helps structure finance correctly, maintain borrowing power, and secure favourable mortgage products.
- Estate agents provide market insight, access to deals, and early information when strong relationships are built.
- A qualified surveyor identifies structural or valuation risks before purchase, preventing unexpected costs
- A solicitor or conveyancer protects your interests, manages legal processes, handles contracts, and prevents hidden risks.
- An experienced accountant ensures tax efficiency, proper structuring, compliance, and long term financial planning.
- A competent property manager/letting agent handles tenants, maintenance, rent collection, and compliance, freeing the investor from day to day issues.
- Mentors or experienced investors accelerate learning by sharing practical insights, networks, and guidance.
- Cutting corners by choosing cheap service providers often leads to higher costs later; quality pays for itself in property.
- The right team doesn't just support success—they multiply it by ensuring smooth transactions, informed decisions, and sustainable portfolio growth.

Chapter 12 The Numbers That Tell The Story

"Every property has a story — it tells it in numbers."

INTRODUCTION: WHY NUMBERS MATTER

Every successful investment has two sides — the vision and the valuation. The vision gets you started, but the valuation keeps you grounded. Property investment is as much about numbers as it is about bricks, people, or places. The numbers tell the story behind every decision, every opportunity, and every success.

Understanding the numbers gives you clarity. It tells you if a deal makes sense, if the return is worth the risk, and whether your investment will stand the test of time. In this chapter, I'll walk you through some real examples from my own property journey. These aren't theories; they are lessons written in profit, patience, and experience.

Each property you own should have its own story, one that begins with sound research, is sustained by disciplined numbers, and ends with either profit or learning. I have come to view losses not as failures, but as the cost of education, sometimes an expensive lesson. My hope is that this book, and this section in particular, will equip you with the knowledge needed to shorten that learning curve and help you avoid unnecessary losses.

CASE STUDY 1: MY FIRST PROPERTY – THE BEGINNING OF A JOURNEY

The property was a two-bedroom split-level apartment—modest in size but rich in potential. I purchased it for £50,500, putting down a 5% deposit of £2,525 and borrowing £47,975. I financed the purchase with an endowment mortgage, with an interest rate of around 6.59%, and within a few months I had my first tenant in place.

The rent was £650 per month, giving me a gross rental income of approximately £7,800 per year. The annual mortgage interest came to around £3,160, and once I added the endowment premium and other running costs, my total annual expenses were roughly £4,600. This left me with a modest but reliable cash flow of around £260 per month before tax.

When I ran the numbers, the gross yield worked out at approximately 15.4%, while the net yield came in at around 6.3% after expenses. But the real turning point came later. As the property increased in value over time, I realised I could leverage the equity to help fund the purchase of my next property setting the foundations for portfolio growth.

That first deal wasn't perfect. I made mistakes, learned on the job, and didn't fully understand the tax or management side. But it worked. It taught me that property wasn't just about ownership it was about using assets to create opportunity.

Lesson learned: Start where you are, learn as you go, and let your first property teach you what no course can.

CASE STUDY 2: THE QUICK WIN - £500 DEPOSIT THAT TURNED INTO £46,100 PROFIT

This story remains one of my favourite examples of what I call a "quick win."

Background: I visited a large new-build development in Enfield, Middlesex, hoping to secure a unit. The sales team informed me that all the properties in that phase of the development had already been sold. Before leaving, they asked me to leave my contact details to be kept informed of the new phase, which I did.

Opportunity: A few days later, I received a call from the salesperson. A buyer had pulled out of a purchase, and they asked if I was still interested. They explained that they would honour the original price agreed with the previous buyer, even though the next phase would be released at a higher price. Initially, I thought it might be a marketing gimmick, because I had heard of such situations in large developments. Yet, I took the gamble and paid the £500 non-refundable deposit. It turned out to be a wise decision!

Execution: Within weeks, I secured a mortgage, instructed a solicitor, and exchanged contracts with delayed completion. Later, I was asked to come in to pick my choice of tiles, kitchen build etc. The house was scheduled to be completed months later. As a single man at the time, I didn't need a three-bedroom house, and with high interest rates and a weak rental market for new builds at that time, I decided to sell instead. Before legal completion, my estate agent started to market the property and found an interested buyer and arranged a back-to-back completion.

The idea that you can sell a property that you didn't quite own (although I had exchanged contracts, with huge penalties if I pulled out of the sale, so technically it was mine) was new to me. My solicitor coordinated both transactions so that the buyer's funds were used to settle my purchase. The previous mortgage that I had applied for ended before it started! I never spent a single night in the house, and my capital (deposit) was tied up for only a brief period.

Result: By the time the property was completed, prices had risen significantly. I exited the deal with a profit of £46,100, paid directly into my bank account without managing tenants, handling renovations, or enduring long holding periods.

Lesson Learned: There are quick wins in property, but they aren't always about speed, they're about strategy and timing and sometimes favour! By staying flexible and leveraging back-to-back completion, I turned a £500 deposit into a five-figure profit with minimal effort.

CASE STUDY 3: THE STEADY PERFORMER

Not every property announces its success early, but some demonstrate their value steadily and convincingly over time.

This property was acquired for £125,000 using a 25% deposit, equating to an initial capital investment of approximately £31,250 (excluding acquisition costs), amount realised from refinancing another property. It operates under a guaranteed rent scheme. At the outset, the property generated a guaranteed monthly income of £850. Over time, through contractual uplifts and sustained tenant demand, this increased to approximately £1,050 per month.

To get a snapshot of its performance over a ten-year period, average rental income was approximately £950 per month, or £11,400 per annum. Measured against the purchase price, the initial gross rental yield was approximately 8.2%, rising to around 10.1% as rents increased. After accounting for mortgage payments, management fees, insurance, and maintenance totalling roughly £4,500 per year, the property continued to deliver consistent net income.

Alongside income, the underlying asset strengthened materially. Over the same timeframe, the property's market value increased from £125,000 to approximately £250,000. While neither income nor capital growth followed a straight line, the combined effect of time, demand, and disciplined ownership was substantial.

This example illustrates the power of secured income and responsible leverage. What appears steady on a monthly basis can be genuinely impressive when viewed across a longer horizon.

Lesson learned: Property wealth is built quietly through structure and patience. When income is stabilised and assets are allowed time to perform, the results speak for themselves.

CASE STUDY 4: PRIORITISING CASH FLOW OVER CAPITAL GROWTH

When investing in property, it is essential to understand not only the asset itself and its location, but also the purpose it is intended to serve. Every acquisition should be aligned with a clearly defined objective. Several years ago, I purchased a two-bedroom apartment in an economically deprived area of a Northern Ireland city for £33,500. At the time, my priority was high rental income, with the specific aim of replacing earned income. That objective shaped both the type of property I pursued and the location in which I invested. While it is sometimes possible to find assets that deliver both strong capital growth and high income, in practice many investments favour one over the other, requiring deliberate trade-offs.

The low purchase price reflected local socio-economic challenges, the fact that the property required light renovation, and limited lender appetite at the time. The price only marginally exceeded the £25,000 minimum property value accepted by many mortgage providers, which significantly reduced competition.

I acquired the property with a 25 percent deposit (£8,375) and financed the remaining £25,125, representing an initial loan-to-value ratio of approximately 75 per cent. Despite the area's challenges, strong local ties created consistent demand for affordable rental accommodation.

Thirteen years later, the apartment is valued at approximately £60,000, representing a capital increase of £26,500, or around 79 per cent on the original purchase price. While this appreciation is modest when compared with higher-growth markets elsewhere in the UK, capital growth was not the primary objective. Importantly, the increase in value has reduced the effective loan-to-value ratio to approximately 42 per cent, materially strengthening the asset's risk profile.

From an income perspective, the property has performed strongly. It currently generates £700 per month, or £8,400 per year, producing a gross yield of approximately 25 per cent on the original purchase price (£8,400 ÷ £33,500). When measured against the initial cash invested, the result is even more striking: the annual rental income broadly matches the original deposit, equating to a cash-on-cash return of around 100 percent per annum before costs.

Even when assessed against its current valuation, the property continues to deliver a robust income return, with rental income representing approximately 14 per cent of today's value (£8,400 ÷ £60,000). In practical terms, the original capital invested was effectively recovered through rental income within the first year of stabilised letting.

This example illustrates a central principle of disciplined property investing: success is not defined by headline capital growth alone, but by how effectively an asset delivers against its intended purpose. Knowing whether an investment is designed to prioritise income, capital growth, or a balance of both is essential to making sound, sustainable decisions over the long term.

CASE STUDY 5: MY BIGGEST MISTAKE - THE PRICE OF IMPATIENCE

No investor's journey is without challenges. This case study is not about numbers but more about the wrong decisions that I made along the way. This purchase was an emotional purchase, and although the figure looked good, my impatience cost me thousands of pounds!

This property was a good deal. It was in a strong location, it needed work, and I believed there was clear potential of adding value and forcing up the valuation and the returns. However, I also wanted the property for personal reasons, and that clouded my judgment. I was determined to buy it at all costs and bring it to market in record time, and in doing so, I made several rookie mistakes.

My original intention was to finance the purchase with a mortgage. The bank carried out a basic valuation survey, which the property passed. Unfortunately, the mortgage did not proceed because the seller had agreed to sell to me at a price lower than the bank's valuation, and this created complications the lender was unwilling to accept. Rather than stepping back, I pushed ahead.

I decided to raise funds and purchase the property outright in cash. Because the property required a full renovation and the purchase was no longer subject to a mortgage, I completed the transaction without commissioning a full structural survey, relying instead on the bank's basic valuation report. That decision proved costly.

After the purchase, serious structural issues came to light. Before any renovation work could begin, I had to invest significant time and money resolving these problems. Eager to recover lost time and get the property to market, I made another mistake. In my rush, I began making structural changes to the property before securing full planning permission for the change I wanted to make to the property.

Although I had initial discussions with the local council and was advised informally that the proposal was unlikely to face objections, the formal planning process required consultation with neighbouring residents. A coordinated objection emerged within the neighbourhood, supported by a local councillor who lived nearby, and the council ultimately rejected my application based a technicality.

I was left with no choice but to reverse the unauthorised changes and return the property to its original use, incurring further cost, delay, and frustration.

Lesson Learned: Never allow emotion or urgency to override due diligence. Always commission the appropriate surveys, especially when buying without mortgage oversight. Secure full planning permission before carrying out structural changes, regardless of informal assurances. Property rewards patience, preparation, and discipline and penalises shortcuts and I was severally penalised!

CASE STUDY 6: INTEREST-ONLY OR REPAYMENT

One of the most debated decisions in property investment is whether to use a repayment mortgage or an interest-only mortgage. Both approaches can be rational, and both can be powerful when aligned with an investor's objectives, time horizon, and discipline.

This question is specific to property investors rather than residential owner occupiers. For most homeowners, fully repaying a mortgage and living debt free is a sensible goal, as their primary residence is exposed in the event of default.

For investors, the context is different. The investment property itself serves as the collateral securing the loan. This means that, in the event of repossession, the investment asset is at risk rather than the investor's home. Within this framework, the decision becomes a strategic one rather than an emotional one.

The question, therefore, is not which option is universally better, but which structure is most appropriate for the strategy being pursued. I personally love the idea of repayment, but it is not always possible for cash flow reasons and other financial priorities. See below for a balanced argument.

THE CASE FOR REPAYMENT MORTGAGES

Certainty, Discipline, and Guaranteed Progress

A repayment mortgage steadily reduces the loan balance over an agreed term. Each monthly payment includes both interest and capital, meaning the debt declines predictably until it is fully extinguished.

The greatest strength of a repayment mortgage lies in certainty. Regardless of market conditions, the investor knows that the loan will be cleared by a specific date. This removes refinancing risk and ensures that equity is built even in stagnant or falling markets.

The Mathematics of Repayment (Illustrative)

Consider a £100,000 mortgage over 25 years at 5 per cent interest.

- Monthly repayment is approximately £585
- Total paid over the term is approximately £175,500
- The capital is fully repaid at the end of the term

While the total interest cost is significant, the investor finishes with an unencumbered asset. There is no reliance on future values, refinancing availability, or external discipline. Repayment mortgages also impose forced saving. Capital reduction happens automatically, which can be valuable for investors who prefer structure over optionality.

Where Repayment Excels

- Long-term, lower-risk ownership
- Investors approaching retirement
- Lower tolerance for refinancing or interest-rate risk
- A desire for guaranteed debt elimination

THE CASE FOR INTEREST-ONLY MORTGAGES

Cash Flow, Flexibility, and Inflation at Work

With an interest-only mortgage, the borrower pays only the interest on the loan, leaving the capital balance unchanged unless it is voluntarily reduced. The immediate advantage of this structure is improved cash flow. Monthly payments are lower, which can enhance affordability, increase surplus income, and allow capital to be deployed elsewhere in pursuit of additional opportunities.

Using the same £100,000 loan at 5 per cent interest, the monthly interest-only payment is approximately £417, while the capital balance remains £100,000.

The £168 per month difference between repayment and interest-only payments can be redirected into additional property deposits, used for selective overpayments, or invested into other income-producing assets, depending on the investor's wider strategy.

INFLATION: THE SILENT ALLY OF INTEREST-ONLY DEBT

One of the most under-appreciated forces in the repayment versus interest-only debate is inflation. Inflation erodes the real value of money over time. When a loan is fixed in nominal terms, inflation gradually reduces the real burden of that debt.

Consider a £100,000 interest-only mortgage at 5 per cent interest. The monthly payment is approximately £417, and the loan balance remains £100,000 throughout the term. On paper, nothing changes. In real terms, however, the position evolves significantly.

If inflation averages 3 per cent per year, the purchasing power of £100,000 would fall to approximately £74,000 after ten years and to around £55,000 after twenty years. The nominal debt remains unchanged, but its real economic weight is substantially reduced.

If rents increase broadly in line with inflation, a property producing £1,000 per month today could generate approximately £1,340 per month after ten years and around £1,800 per month after twenty years. The mortgage payment remains broadly unchanged, while the income servicing it rises steadily. What initially felt like a meaningful commitment becomes progressively easier to manage.

However, this advantage is not without risk. Over a 25-year mortgage term, interest rates are unlikely to remain constant. If rates rise from 5 per cent to 7 per cent, the monthly interest-only payment on a £100,000 loan would increase from approximately £417 to around £583. At 8 per cent, it would rise further to approximately £667 per month. While inflation and rent growth may offset some of this increase, higher rates can compress cash flow, particularly in the earlier years.

Under a repayment mortgage, rising interest rates also increase monthly payments, but the borrower benefits from a steadily reducing loan balance. As capital is repaid, exposure to future rate increases diminishes over time, providing a degree of built-in risk reduction.

This comparison highlights the trade-off clearly. Interest-only borrowing benefits from inflation and flexibility, but it remains sensitive to interest-rate movements over long periods. Repayment borrowing offers certainty and gradual risk reduction, but at the cost of higher monthly outgoings from the outset.

A FALSE BINARY: THE HYBRID REALITY

In practice, many experienced investors use hybrid approaches. These may include starting on an interest-only basis and switching to repayment later, making periodic lump-sum capital reductions, or using repayment on some properties while maintaining interest-only borrowing on others.

This allows cash flow optimisation in the early years, risk reduction over time, and flexibility for strategy to evolve with life stage.

FRAMING THE DECISION CORRECTLY

The real debate is not repayment versus interest-only. It is a question of certainty versus flexibility, forced discipline versus optional discipline, and debt elimination versus capital deployment.

Neither option is inherently virtuous or reckless. Each amplifies different behaviours and leads to different outcomes.

LESSON LEARNED

Debt structure should serve strategy, not ideology. Repayment mortgages buy certainty. Interest-only mortgages buy flexibility. The wiser investor understands both the benefit and the responsibility of each.

CLOSING REFLECTION

Numbers never lie: they reveal the story behind every property, every decision, and every outcome. But while numbers guide your choices, they don't tell the whole story. Behind every figure is a moment of courage, a calculated risk, and a lesson in persistence and patience.

As you grow in your property journey, don't fear the maths, embrace it. Learn to read the story your numbers are telling. Each deal, whether a win or a lesson, adds a new chapter to your financial independence. In property, progress often begins with a single calculation and the courage to act on what it tells you. In addition, I have come to understand that there will always be another property deal. If you feel off about it, then listen to your instinct.

CHAPTER SUMMARY

This chapter reveals an essential truth about property investing: your success is written in the numbers. Emotions, assumptions, and enthusiasm may get you started, but numbers decide whether an investment is truly working. Across the case studies in this chapter, several powerful lessons emerge—principles that apply to every investor, regardless of experience.

KEY POINTS

- Every property tells a story — and numbers never lie. Numbers reveal the real health of an investment by showing the truth about cash flow, leverage, growth, and risks. They remove emotion and keep your decisions disciplined.
- Start small, learn fast. Your first property doesn't need to be perfect — it just needs to teach you. Even a modest investment can produce strong returns and valuable experience.
- Quick wins come from preparation, not luck. Big profits happen when you respond fast, understand the opportunity, and have strong relationships — not because of luck.
- Steady performers build long-term wealth. Some properties grow quietly in the background, generating reliable income and strong long-term results without drama.
- Cash flow vs. capital growth — know your strategy. Different properties deliver different outcomes; some give strong monthly income while others grow slowly in value, so choose based on your goals.
- Longterm thinking is the real wealth builder. Investors who think in years and decades win because discipline compounds over time, turning small efforts into significant wealth.

Enjoying this book?

I've created a free Property Investor Starter Pack exclusively for readers. It includes helpful tools and spreadsheets that you can use to analyse deals. Download it free at:
BuildWealthThroughProperty.com/start

Chapter 13
Buying Your First Home

"The first home is not about perfection; it's about progress." – Anonymous

For most people who would become property investors, owning your own home rather than paying a landlord would most probably be the right thing for you to do, unless of course, there is a very good reason, like when I lived almost rent free with my aunt (one of my favourite and kindest aunties). There are also those who travel a lot, who might decide not to purchase their own home but rather rent. Regardless, whenever you come to purchase your first property, this chapter will be helpful.

Buying your first home is a milestone moment. It's exciting, emotional, and it can be slightly intimidating. I remember feeling a mix of excitement, anticipation, and uncertainty, wondering whether I was making the "right" choice or missing something obvious. I was glad that I didn't get stuck with analysis paralysis. I was well informed and it worked out for me. What I've learned since is that buying your first home isn't about perfection; it's about preparation, understanding the process, and making informed decisions.

This chapter is here to guide you through that journey from sorting your mortgage to confidently choosing the right property.

START WITH THE NUMBERS, NOT THE PROPERTY

Before you fall in love with a kitchen or a bay window, it's important to get clear on your finances. Most first-time buyers need a mortgage and understanding how it works early on will save you time, stress, and costly mistakes later.

A mortgage is a loan secured against the property you're buying. You repay it over an agreed term—usually 25 to 35 years—with interest charged on the outstanding balance. It's worth remembering that mortgages are a major source of profit for banks, as they earn significant returns from the interest you pay over time.

Because this is a residential home, it's generally in your best interest to overpay your mortgage whenever possible and pay off the debt as soon as you can. The previous discussion on interest-only or repayment mortgages is often in the context of an investment where the income pays the loan interest. Even small overpayments can reduce the loan term and significantly cut the total interest you pay over the life of the mortgage. The earlier you make these overpayments, the greater the impact. That said, some mortgage products—such as fixed-rate mortgages—limit how much you can overpay without incurring penalties, so always check the terms of your agreement.

Because the loan is secured against the property, interest rates are typically lower than those on unsecured borrowing. The trade-off is responsibility: if repayments are not met, the lender has the legal right to repossess the property. This is why affordability—not just how much you can borrow—really matters.

THE PURCHASE JOURNEY, EXPLAINED SIMPLY

Your mortgage journey typically unfolds like this: the first step is securing an Agreement in Principle (AIP) or Decision in Principle (DIP). This is a conditional statement from a lender showing how much they may be willing to lend based on your income, credit profile, and financial commitments. The financial adviser or mortgage adviser I mentioned as part of your power team will conduct the search for suitable lenders. This is where having an experienced, whole-of-market mortgage broker adds real value, as they understand lender criteria and can position your application correctly from the outset. While it is not a guarantee, it gives you a realistic budget to work within, helps you avoid viewing unsuitable properties, and shows estate agents that you are a serious and credible buyer.

With your AIP in place, you can begin searching for a property. This is an important phase, as your chosen property will ultimately determine whether the mortgage is approved. At this stage, your estate agent becomes a key member of your wider property team, helping you identify suitable homes, arrange viewings, and advise on realistic pricing in the local market. Once you find a suitable home and your offer is accepted, the formal mortgage application begins. It is at this stage that you instruct a solicitor. Your estate agent will be at hand to recommend one if you don't already have one, though it is always wise to ensure your solicitor has experience in residential property transactions.

The lender carries out a valuation and underwriting process. The valuation confirms that the property is worth the agreed price and is suitable security for the loan. Underwriting involves detailed checks on your finances to ensure you can comfortably afford the repayments. Some buyers also choose to engage a surveyor at this point to carry out an independent survey, providing reassurance on the condition of the property beyond the lender's basic valuation.

The final step is legal work and completion. Your solicitor conducts searches, reviews contracts, and manages the transfer of ownership. Once everything is signed and funds are released, the purchase completes and you receive the keys to your new home.

Throughout the process, ask questions and stay engaged. If something doesn't make sense, pause and get clarity before moving forward. Buying property is rarely a solo effort, and leaning on the right professionals at the right time can prevent costly mistakes. A confident buyer is an informed buyer.

PROPERTY SEARCHING: WHERE MOST FIRST-TIME BUYERS BEGIN

The best place to start your search is online. There are many websites that are helpful; they allow you to filter by budget, location, size, and property type. I strongly recommend setting up instant alerts, so you're notified the moment something suitable comes onto the market. That said, don't rely solely on websites. Some of the best opportunities never make it online.

WHY ESTATE AGENTS STILL MATTER

Register with estate agents in the areas you're interested in. Pick up the phone or walk into their offices. Let them know that you're a first-time buyer, you have an AIP, and you're ready to move quickly. Estate agents are more likely to engage proactively when they know you are financially prepared and supported by the right advisers.

When agents know you're organised and serious, they're far more likely to keep you in mind when new properties come in sometimes even before they're advertised.

CHOOSING THE RIGHT AREA (NOT JUST THE RIGHT HOUSE)

When buying your first home, particularly a family home, location is just as important as the property itself sometimes more so. One of the important things to look out for is schools. Even if you don't have children, good schools matter. Properties near well-rated schools tend to hold value better and are easier to sell in the future.

Another important amenity is good transport links. Access to trains, buses, and major roads can make a huge difference to daily life and the long-term value of your property.

Other important amenities to look out for include supermarkets, cafés, gyms, parks, GP surgeries, and green spaces. All of these add to quality of life and desirability, which feeds back into the value of your property. I also always recommend visiting the neighbourhood at different times of the day. A street that feels quiet and pleasant at noon can feel very different in the evening.

I remember many years ago when I was searching for a family home. I had identified a property in the Dartford area that met my criteria and viewed it with the estate agent. Later, I decided to visit the area in the evening. Coincidentally, a local police officer stopped me for a routine check.

After the check, and just before he left, I asked for his opinion of the area. I explained that I was considering moving there and mentioned the street in question. Suffice it to say, his feedback was enough to stop me from proceeding.

FUTURE POTENTIAL

For the savvy buyer, it is also important to be aware of any regeneration plans, infrastructure investment, or new developments that may be taking place in the area in the foreseeable future. These factors can significantly enhance an area over time.

Finding Value: Don't Fear a "Tired" Property

One of the most valuable lessons I learned early on was not to be discouraged by cosmetic flaws. If you are reasonably handy or willing to learn, a property that is structurally sound but visually dated can represent excellent value. Worn carpets, faded paint, and outdated kitchens often put buyers off, yet these are usually among the cheapest and simplest issues to address.

With relatively modest effort, a home can be transformed. A fresh coat of paint, new flooring, updated lighting, or a minor refresh to the kitchen or bathroom can dramatically change the feel of a property and add real value without significant cost. Unfortunately, many first-time buyers overlook these opportunities because they are searching for perfection from day one.

Rather than seeing tired houses or apartments as problems, it can be far more helpful to view them as a blank canvas. They offer the freedom to shape the space according to your own taste and lifestyle, allowing you to leave a personal mark on the property while building value at the same time.

Know When to Walk Away

While cosmetic issues can be opportunities, structural problems are a different story. Always get a survey and take it seriously. Damp, roofing issues, or structural movement can quickly turn a "bargain" into a financial headache. If something doesn't feel right, trust your instincts and the survey report. There will always be another property. It is sometimes difficult to walk away because you are so emotionally invested that you always want to make it work.

THE ROLE OF DISCIPLINE (BEFORE AND AFTER YOU BUY)

Strong financial habits don't end once your mortgage is approved. They become even more important after completion. I learned the hard way how a small, missed payment of just £15 can damage your credit and affect future borrowing. That experience stayed with me and shaped how I approach money to this day. Remember that borrowing for investment is leverage! Discipline isn't about restriction; it's about freedom and control.

CAUTION

Your first home does not need to be your forever home. It needs to be affordable, well-located, and right for where you are now. By understanding mortgages, searching smartly, focusing on location, and being open to value-adding opportunities, you can make a confident, informed first step onto the property ladder.

CONCLUSION

Property has endured not because markets are kind, but because its foundations are structural rather than speculative. Land is finite. Shelter is essential. Time rewards ownership. These realities have outlasted policies, recessions, and cycles of fear and enthusiasm.

This book has not argued that property is effortless or without risk. It has argued something more important: that when approached with discipline, patience, and stewardship, property remains one of the most reliable vehicles for building long-term security and wealth.

The difference between those who succeed and those who struggle is rarely timing. It is understanding. Those who respect the numbers, plan conservatively, and think in decades rather than months allow time to do the heavy lifting.

You do not need to start big. You need to start wisely. One well-chosen decision, made with clarity and held with discipline, compounds quietly over years

Property rewards those who treat it not as a shortcut, but as a system. If you do that, you will find that while markets rise and fall, the fundamentals remain and over time, they work in your favour.

CHAPTER SUMMARY

This chapter guides first-time buyers through the home-buying process with clarity and confidence. While owning is generally more beneficial than renting, personal circumstances matter. Buying a first home can be exciting yet intimidating, so preparation and informed decision-making are key. Success comes from practical, well-considered choices rather than perfection. The chapter begins by emphasising the importance of understanding your finances, borrowing responsibly, and making early mortgage overpayments where possible to reduce long-term interest and strengthen financial security.

KEY POINTS

The Mortgage Journey. The process begins with obtaining an Agreement in Principle, which sets a clear budget and builds credibility with sellers. Working with an experienced mortgage broker helps you find the right lender and ensures a smooth application process.

- **Understanding the Buying Process.** Buying a home involves brokers, estate agents, solicitors, and surveyors. Staying engaged, asking questions, and relying on expert guidance helps avoid costly mistakes.
- **Searching Effectively.** Online property portals are a good starting point, but relationships with local estate agents are equally important. Being organised, mortgage-ready, and proactive improves your chances of securing the right property.
- **Prioritise Location.** Location matters more than the property itself for long-term value. Schools, transport links, amenities, and neighbourhood quality should be key factors in your decision.
- **Look for Value, Not Perfection.** Cosmetic issues can present opportunities to add value. A structurally sound but dated property can be improved over time and may offer better long-term potential than a finished home.

- **Know When to Walk Away.** Cosmetic problems are manageable, but structural issues can be costly. A professional survey is essential, and disciplined buyers must be willing to step back when necessary.
- **Financial Discipline.** Good financial habits remain vital after purchase. Protecting your credit, budgeting carefully, and managing repayments safeguard future borrowing power.
- **Final Reminder.** Your first home does not need to be your forever home. It should be affordable, well located, and suited to your current stage of life, creating a foundation for future growth.

Appendix A: Mortgage Types and Financing Structures

COMMON MORTGAGE TYPES

Generally speaking, there are several types of mortgages, each with distinct features and conditions:

- **Tracker Mortgages**
  Interest rates track a central bank rate, such as the Bank of England base rate, and move up or down accordingly.
- **Standard Variable Rate (SVR)**
  A lender's default rate, which can fluctuate at their discretion.
- **Discounted Rate Mortgages**
  Offer a temporary discount on the lender's SVR for a fixed period.
- **Offset Mortgages**
  Link savings or current accounts to the mortgage balance, reducing interest payable.
- **Interest-Only Mortgages**
  Monthly payments cover interest only, with the capital repaid at the end of the term.
- **Buy-to-Let Mortgages**
  Designed for rental properties. Often interest-only, but repayment options also exist.
- **Help-to-Buy Mortgages**
  Government-backed schemes aimed at assisting first-time buyers with smaller deposits.

Appendix B: Alternative Forms of Leverage

Beyond traditional mortgages, investors may access leverage through the following methods:

- **Home Equity Loans**
  Borrowing against existing property equity, often used to fund deposits for further purchases.
- **Home Equity Line of Credit (HELOC)**
  A revolving credit facility secured against property equity.
- **Seller Financing**
  The seller provides finance directly to the buyer, bypassing traditional lenders.
- **Private Money Lenders**
  Individuals or groups offering fast access to capital, typically at higher interest rates.
- **Real Estate Investment Trusts (REITs)**
  Provide indirect exposure to property through pooled investment structures.
- **Syndication**
  Multiple investors combining capital to fund larger projects.
- **Cross-Collateralisation**
  Using equity from one property to secure financing on another.

Appendix C: Key UK Property Regulations and Government Measures

- **Stamp Duty Land Tax (SDLT)**
  A surcharge applies to second homes and investment properties, introduced to curb speculative buying.
- **Help to Buy Scheme**
  Launched in 2013 to assist first-time buyers with equity loans on new-build properties.
- **Tenant Fees Act (2019)**
  Prohibits landlords and agents from charging most upfront tenant fees.
- **Permitted Development Rights (PDR)**
  Allow certain property conversions without full planning permission.

Appendix D: Limited Company Ownership (SPV Structures)

Who Should Consider a Limited Company

A company structure may be suitable if you:

- Are a higher- or additional-rate taxpayer
- Plan to build a multi-property portfolio
- Intend to reinvest profits rather than withdraw them
- Are planning for inheritance and succession
- Use interest-only mortgage structures

Who Should Not Use a Limited Company

Personal ownership may be preferable if you:

- Are a basic-rate taxpayer
- Plan to own only one property
- Need rental income for personal living costs
- Prefer simplicity and minimal administration
- Intend to trade properties frequently

Appendix E: Popular Property Search Websites

United Kingdom

England & Wales:

Rightmove, Zoopla, OnTheMarket, PrimeLocation

Scotland:

Rightmove, Zoopla, ESPC, s1homes

Northern Ireland:

PropertyPal, PropertyNews, Rightmove

References

BBC One (2009–2015) *Rogue Traders.* Television programme. London: British Broadcasting Corporation.

Channel 5 (2008–2009) *Cowboy Builders.* Television programme. London: Channel 5 Television Corporation.

HM Courts & Tribunals Service (n.d.) *County Court judgments (CCJs).* Available at: https://www.gov.uk/county-court-judgments-ccj-for-debt (Accessed: 14 January 2026).

HM Land Registry and Office for National Statistics (n.d.) *UK House Price Index (UK HPI).* Available at: https://www.gov.uk/government/collections/uk-house-price-index-reports (Accessed: 22/02/2026).

HM Revenue & Customs (2020) *Restriction of finance cost relief for individual landlords.* Available at: gov.uk (Accessed: 14 January 2026).

HM Revenue & Customs (2023) *Property income and company taxation.* Available at: gov.uk (Accessed: 14 January 2026).

Housing Act 1988 (1988) *Housing Act 1988: Section 8.* London: HMSO.

Nationwide Building Society (n.d.) *UK House Price Index – Real House Prices Series.* Available at: https://www.nationwide.co.uk/house-price-index/ (Accessed: 22/02/2026).

Nationwide Building Society (n.d.) *UK House Price Index.* Available at: https://www.nationwide.co.uk/house-price-index/ (Accessed: [insert date]).

Office for National Statistics (2024) *Consumer Price Inflation.* London: ONS. Available at: Office for National Statistics publications (Accessed: Day Month Year).

Private Tenancies (Northern Ireland) Order 2006 (2006) *Private Tenancies (Northern Ireland) Order 2006*. Belfast: HMSO.

Private Housing (Tenancies) (Scotland) Act 2016 (2016) *Private Housing (Tenancies) (Scotland) Act 2016*. Edinburgh: The Scottish Government.

Royal Institution of Chartered Surveyors (RICS) (2023) *Residential management code (3rd edition)*. Available at: rics.org (Accessed: 14 January 2026).

Made in the USA
Monee, IL
13 September 2026

62975582R00095